Jack R.
Box 54.
—upara Tex.
78016

Please write me

My New Life

—A Spiritual Odyssey—

With an emphasis on:
Chattahoochee-
And
Faith Gospel Mission to-
(Native American Indians, Cuba, and Mexico)

Includes selected excerpts from the

Journal of Rev. Thomas Griffin (1787—1851)

By:

Jack Ray Griffin

&

Robert Silas Griffin

Donations accepted

xulon
PRESS

Dedication

I dedicate my biography first, to my wife Anna Adele. Secondly, to all the survivors of Chattahoochee with a special regard to Kenneth Donaldson and Chris Calhoun who were catalysts for change in a corrupt system. I also include in my dedicatory, Phillip L. Cooper and the one known convert to Christianity during my stay at Chattahoochee. Above all, I dedicate My New Life to the memory of the appreciable Christian life and wide-ranging ministry of Rev. Thomas Griffin. He was born 1787, in Cumberland County, Virginia and died about 1851 in Madison County, Mississippi. He was appointed by Methodist Bishop Francis Asbury along with three of his contemporary ministers to be circuit riding preachers. Thomas Griffin served the Lord Jesus Christ as a faithful soldier of the cross traveling and evangelizing in 18 states from South Carolina to Texas and from Canada to Florida. As a "Saddlebags" preacher and later as a Presiding Elder, he became known as the "Boanerges" of the Southwestern United States and Territories. He also was a farmer with a family to care for and he traveled by means of walking and carrying his things, on horseback, on mules, sometimes by swimming or carried by currents. Often, he traversed the country in pirogues, rafts and canoes in swamps, by steam boats and keelboats on rivers, creeks and canals, in stagecoaches, on railroads, and in hacks or buggies. New genealogical and historical information comes from his Day Book and Journal dating from 1841, which has never been published in its entirety. Our beloved Griffin ancestor set an example of how we should follow in the footsteps of Jesus of Galilee. By God's Grace we can also follow in the footsteps of Jesus and make heaven our home.

Francis Asbury was born 1745, in England. During his 45 years of exemplary Christian ministry in America, he traveled 270,000 miles and preached 16,000 sermons. As Bishop and Superintendent of the Wesleyan Societies in America, he ordained Thomas Griffin as an evangelical missionary. He once said: *"My desire is to live in love and peace with all men; to do them no harm, but all the good I can. The Lord will provide for those who trust in Him"*.

—Jack R. Griffin, June 2006

"Follow peace with all men, and Holiness, without which no one shall see the Lord." (Hebrews 12: 14)

Author's Note

The primary purpose of this book is to evidence as clearly and plainly as possible, that there is a reality in knowing and serving the Lord Jesus Christ. I also desire that people realize that there is a very great difference between mere religion and true spiritual Christianity. Humanity has fallen into a dreadful and sinful state which requires an intervention called redemption. There is hope for humanity in Christ. My New Life story is written in order to present the clearest possible evidence that Christianity is founded on Jesus Christ, the only Son of God and sole Savior of all who believe on His name. I do not wish to promote any conflict between people, denominations or religions by presenting the simple Divine plan of intervention. It is of paramount importance to know and to recognize that our main purpose in this life is to prepare for the life to come so that we may safely dwell for eternity in the Celestial City of God.

Let each one of us examine ourselves to make sure we have been washed in the blood of Jesus, Born-Again according to the Word of God, and Saved by Grace through Faith unto good works. This is the simple plan of God for the human race and it is my simple desire and prayer as well. Please allow God to intervene in your life.

—*Jack Ray Griffin, Evangelist*

Contents

Foreword

By God's Grace; I have had sufficient time to grow up and reflect upon the past, savor the present and ponder the future. Looking back, now I can better understand what happened in many situations in my life and in my family. I have but one regret; I should have become a Christian much sooner. The years I have done Evangelical Missionary work with my Dad in the United States and in Mexico was time well spent. I consider it to be one of my life's greatest accomplishments to be my Dad's biographer. It is quite revealing to sketch a human interest story and flesh out a person's life that is fast approaching a century in duration. I am neither an apologist nor a polemicist. However, as a historian, historical re-enactor and history teacher, I clearly see the intimate relativity of God and humanity in the historical records and I present the facts.

A great uncle- Rev. Thomas Griffin wrote an interesting segment in his journal on May 22, 1841, concerning Napoleon and his condition after Waterloo: *"Sir Hudson Lowe was selected by the English government to see those rebellious were faithfully executed.* (While governor of St. Helena from 1815 to 1821, Sir Hudson Lowe served as the custodian of Napoleon I) *Napoleon avowed he believed the English intended to kill him by their treatment and Lowe was the instrument to accomplish their diabolical designs. Sir Hudson Lowe replied: "If you believe that, you do not know us." "Know you," replied Napoleon, "How should I know you, what have you done to make yourself known? Men are known by their acts".* (Griffin, p.

21) If the temporal British government can at one time in its history hold a self-crowned, continental emperor to strict accounting for deeds committed and later, the British Crown itself be held to colonial accounts in India by a half-robed man of small stature with a bamboo cane in one hand known as Mahatma Ghandi, how much more can the Almighty God, Creator of the earth and the universe, hold each one of us to an exact accounting for all our deeds done in this life? God's Great White Throne Judgment is surely a promise to be fulfilled for the reprehensible sinner and all the wicked.

In light of the record of pseudo-scientific ideas and junk science ad-nauseam, useless to humanity from inception, I can only say the philosophy of assessing personality to assess character and subsequently judging the value of a human being on the basis of pseudo-scientific methods involved in such assessments, is definitely a slippery slope. How many people have been victimized by the fraudulent pseudo-science of phrenology, Piltdown, shoe fitting fluoroscopes and psychographs? How much effort and money has been wasted on the falsehoods of typology, graphology, psychognomy, craniology, lobotomy, and anthropometry? What is the count and the cost of such charlatan, pseudo-scientific "developments" in terms of deception, human suffering, and even lives? The fact is, counterfeit money indicates there is genuine money and it follows that counterfeit religion and pseudo-science are indicative of genuine Christianity and real science. Not everything is bogus and fake but we sure do need to be able to distinguish between the false and the real. In the realm of religion, the Holy Spirit of God must carefully guide the Christian to the truth. To avoid muddled thinking, it is necessary to exercise common sense and to have the gift of spiritual discernment.

I ponder the reasons why and I question the motives of some professionals and relatives directly involved in Dad experiencing the odyssey of Chattahoochee. How well I remember my first visit to Chattahoochee in 1958, and seeing my Dad confined behind cold steel bars in a cell like some dangerous criminal, as one human crumb among many. In my defense of the World's Best Dad, I emphatically declare that I never experienced any type of domestic abuse as a child or as a teenager. My Dad never committed any act in public or in private that warranted involuntary confinement in a place such as Chattahoochee. He, along with many other innocent Americans, could never have belonged in a place where some men and women patients howled and screamed for hours, or the opposites staring for years from empty eyes, while others defecated in their clothing or on the floor, or were kept in straightjackets or penned naked in open-air cages like some species of wild beast. (Donaldson, p. 123) A place where some so-called doctors also screamed in one's face over nothing at all, performing lobotomies in the self-sanctified name of progressive science and modern psychiatry. The standardized remedy for most if not all patients involuntarily confined in Chattahoochee was, more treatment, always more "treatment". It appears that in many cases a "cure" was never delivered unless effected by someone in the free world leveraging a patient out of the repository of human crumbs by virtue of signing a release form, perhaps through a favorable court hearing, by influential political connections in the state or nation's capitol or via a successful law suit in the Supreme Court of the United States of America. The evil trinity of pseudo-psychiatry, pseudo-religion and perverted-justice seemed to have walked hand-in-hand for a time in Florida.

Although the mercenary perpetrators have been forgiven long ago and most have already crossed over the river to their destinies, I will never forget the tragic scene of Dad's involuntary confinement. After doing significant research on the history and social impact of this institution and discovering a book, a website and a film about other Chattahoochee victims and survivors, I decided it was time to help my Dad write his biography. I sincerely hope that this human interest story is one that will inspire and motivate other people to do what is right- in God's eyes. I am fortunate to have visited the Department of Veteran's- Medical Center in Gulfport, Mississippi with my Dad on August 30, 1995. We visited the building where he had lived for a short time, we talked to some of the patients and staff including the Chaplain and we videotaped a live interview of Dad on the grounds. It was also a Blessing to visit Chattahoochee in June 2003, with my Dad, Mom and friends from the Wisham family. We were given an extensive tour of the facility and visited some of the wards that Dad had lived on. Information was found on Dad's Christian friend- Phillip L. Cooper who was committed for the same reason. This time, Dad's chin was up, his spirit was free, and in spite of using a cane, his steps were unconfined. No one tried to detain him or our party, no threat of more "treatment" was tendered and the staff represented some of the friendliest and most accommodating professionals I've met. Change is good. I felt a significant measure of closure and I know my parents did as well as we drove away toward the west as a family and as free people. For the sake of setting the historical record straight for the present and for posterity, it is altogether appropriate to present the biography of a Christian man in the spirit of impartial truth, in the context of family history and in the love of God. — R. Silas Griffin

"Liberty is the prevention of control by others. This requires self-control and, therefore, religious and spiritual influences; education, knowledge, well-being." — <u>Lord Acton</u>

ONE

A Happy Child at Home

The surname Griffin comes from the ancient Welch name of Gryffud and among other definitions, it can be interpreted as meaning "big red". Other variations are Gryffyd, Griff, Griffen, Griffing, and Griffey. A paternal ancestor of our Griffin family emigrated from Wales to the Virginia colony in the 1600's. Based on primary historical sources, our American family began with a Welsh immigrant in the New World, growing into a family tree dedicated to the principles of faith in God, liberty and patriotism to the Constitutional ideals of These United States of America. All of the documented genealogical and historical sources indicate the Griffin family derived from a Protestant-Evangelical European ancestry. My third great-grandfather was John Griffin born September 3, 1740, in Powhatan County, Virginia. He served as a Sergeant in Captain William Earl's 1st North Carolina Regiment, then as Lieutenant, and finally as Capitan under the command of General George Washington during the American Revolution. A son, Thomas Griffin wrote some details concerning our pioneer Griffin lineage in his Journal of 1841. He reveals:

"I was born September 24, 1787, in the County of Cumberland, State of Virginia. I am the youngest but one of eight children raised by marriage between John Griffin and Mary Andrews, both

Virginians. (Of eleven children total, eight must have been living in 1841) *My father's family was of Welch descent, my mother's I have been informed was English. During thirty years observation and treading on the soil of eighteen states and becoming acquainted with many of the names, all I have met with trace their origin to Wales. I will attempt to give a faint description of the Griffins I have met with, admitting some exceptions. Medium in libertys, quick irritable temper by nature. Hard to be driven but can be led, warm friends and warm ways and I am informed that in early years and gone by ages, the old stock if insulted, they instantly avenged themselves according to accurate usages by hard gloves, with the fist, etc. They inherit something of the national character, Wales is now a component part of Great Britain and it is also said the English had much trouble in subjugating or amalgamating them with the nation. My grandfather, David Griffin, as far as I know had only two brothers. One of them was an early adventure to Kentucky and it is said had a family. The other brother removed to the Carolinas and had a family though I know nothing of either.*

My father, (John Griffin) when a grown man, went into the world as I oft heard him say, with nothing but a horse and a saddle. About the year I would judge 1792 or 3, himself, Joseph Hubbert and Robert Smith set out for Georgia. A tremendous undertaking for those days. A-W-A-Y to Georgia, 4 or 5 hundred miles, a frontier state of the United States. My father purchased a tract of land on the Big Creek, 4 miles from the Oconee River now lying in the county of Oglethorpe, 10 miles from Lexington. He was charmed with Georgia, soft and mild was the climate, high and elevated, good water and fresh soil- an inexhaustible stand of timber according to the terms then in use: "Not a stick amiss." The inhabitants plain and utterly friendly to a proverb, making every effort to invite settlers to come in.

His land lay an mile from Capt. Reids Fort and not a house outside of it. The younger branches of the family and mother wast left in the settlement. Himself, 2- sons, a young man and a few servants commenced on his land. He built a strong, hewed log house, chinked and daubed the cracks, leaving places for port holes so this new residence was- residence, block house, fort and hall. He held his ground and made bread that year and not a house there west of him.

Within my recollection, Oglethorpe County should be the outside settlement and my father's house the outside house. There was much troubles such as stealing horses and the family of William Thrasher was killed near the Scull Shoals after father brought us from the old settlement to Big Creek. The next year, the county began to settle up rapidly, log houses was building in every direction and the fields began to be opened. There was but few slaves there then. The people done their own work or it was left undone.

My father had an aversion to the learned pursuits and if his circumstances would have justified it, I believe he would have made us all planters and as he had no fortune to give us externally, he would give us one internally, as such, he learned us to work- and work hard. I continued with my father and worked on the farm until I was 25 years of age. My grand- father and mother, were of the regular Baptist for something like thirty years and I believe they were good people and I hope, died in peace. My father, in theory professed to somewhat believe that way, he would not fully subscribe to the creed. My mother's attachments were to the Methodist people and my father's to the Baptist, the house was divided". (Griffin, p. 25—29, 32, 34, 40)

John Griffin died about 1819, in either Greene or Oglethorpe County, Georgia having fathered and raised at least eleven children including the twins, David Andrews Griffin and Jesse Andrews Griffin. I am descended from David Andrews Griffin, killed along with his twin brother Jesse by Creek Indian "Red Stick" warriors in the Bashi Skirmish of Clarke County, Alabama in the autumn of 1813. The direct paternal lineage from David Griffin and Mary Dearin in Virginia is through their son John Griffin (born 9/3/1740 VA to 1819 GA) who married Mary Ann Andrews, through their son David (born 2/14/1787 VA—1813 AL) who married Susannah (Moore?), through their son William (11/9/1812 AL to 4/20/1868 AL) who married Annie Drinkard, through their son John H. Griffin (5/14/1846 AL to 12/28/1902 AL) who married Lydia Dunning, through their son; my father Ivy Oma Griffin, known to us as "Pop" or "Poppa." Several generations of our Griffin family were dedicated citizens and farmers in the colonies, on the frontiers of several states and territories as well as during part of the Great Depression. Some aspects of the Griffin family history in Alabama, Georgia, Louisiana, and Mississippi are recorded in various publications such as: Clarke County Alabama and its Surroundings by Rev. T. H. Ball, A Complete History of Methodism- Vols. 1 & 2 by Rev. John G. Jones, The Mississippi Territory in the War of 1812, by Mrs. Dunbar Rowland, A History of Methodism by Bishop Holland McTyeire, A Way Through the Wilderness by William C. Davis, The Keelboat Age in Western Waters by Leland D. Baldwin, and Run, Eunice by Kathleen White Schad. Rev. Thomas Griffin's Journal also reveals some details of our family history.

My parents were Mr. Ivy Oma Griffin or "Poppa", born March 13, 1880, and raised near Glover in Clarke County, Alabama and Miss Bashi Leona Keel, born March 2, 1880, also in Clarke County, Alabama. They were married on March 13, 1901, and eventually, a total of eight children were born. In birth order they were: Iree, John Hellis, Oma Quill, Meldee, Jack Ray, Emma Kate, Lovey Dell, and Ivy Byrd. Mother gave birth to me on December 24, 1914, in a rural farm home near grove Hill, Alabama with the invaluable help of an African-American woman midwife. My mother never lost a child and much of the credit goes to the Black midwife who efficiently attended each of our births.

One of the first impressions recorded in my mind was when I was about four years old. I clearly remember making a trip in the fall of 1918, with my next to oldest brother, Oma Quill Griffin, to take about a bale of our own handpicked, loose cotton to be ginned. The nearest cotton gin was at Whatley, Alabama, nine miles away from our farmstead. The round-trip took all day in our sturdy farm wagon with sideboards and pulled by our two mules. These mules were used to plow the fields, pull the family wagon, and for other farm chores. I remember very well what we ate for dinner at the small railroad station community of Whatley. We bought a piece of hoop cheese, some saltine crackers and a couple of cold Nu-Grape soda pops in glass bottles from an icebox. It was very seldom we ever had any cheese to eat in our home and I have always had affection for good cheese. The family cotton pickers at this time were Poppa, Momma, Iree, Hellis, Quill, and Meldee. As each of the Griffin children grew old enough to work in the field, we all eventually picked a heap of cotton. When my turn came to help work in the fields, Momma made a cotton sack with a shoulder strap for me out of an empty 25-pound flour sack. I actually filled this sack completely full of cotton only after I had gained some experience in picking. On one occasion, I was so tired from picking cotton that I lay down on my sack to rest. The next thing I knew Poppa was standing over me with a cotton stalk in his hand and he was saying: *"Get up from there boy and get back to work"*! My Dad was a hard working Alabaman and he didn't have to repeat himself in telling us what to do. Poppa had to rent farmland in Alabama in order to raise crops. I recall that we lived on various homesteads such as the Chatman and Seiglar places. In spite of our Griffin family being very poor all of my life as a child; we lived a happy life at home.

The next event that I recall was when we lived in the corner house at the intersection of roads going to Whatley and Grove Hill where the present day state highways #84 and #43 intersect. I was about six years old and distinctly remember the occasion of the marriage of my oldest sister Iree Griffin to John Armistead in the front room of this house. On a rolling hill behind the house was a pecan orchard and I would pick up gallon-sized buckets of pecans and my Dad would pay me a silver dollar for each gallon of pecans. Later on, I can remember when I started attending school in Grove Hill. My first grade teacher's name was Kling Daisy. Poppa moved around Clarke County, Alabama quite a bit as he farmed and raised his family. I remember when Quill, Meldee and I had to walk three miles to a new brick school in downtown Grove Hill to get an elementary education. Since we only had a farm wagon and a horse-drawn buggy during the time we lived in Alabama, we hardly made any trips other than to Whatley or to Westbend on the Tombigbee River in western Clarke County. This is where I saw my first electric light bulb in the home of my oldest sister Iree and her husband John Armistead. He worked in the engine room on a river tugboat as they pushed barges from the port city of Mobile, up and down the Tombigbee River. John Armistead was a descendant of a Revolutionary War soldier by the name of Captain William Armistead. In Ball's History of Clarke County, Alabama, Captain

Armistead is described as being a native Virginian, a gentleman of the old school, wearing knee buckles and having English tastes. A collateral line of this Armistead family of Virginia produced the famous Confederate Brigadier General Lewis Addison Armistead. He was mortally wounded in leading part of the famous Pickett's Charge at the battle of Gettysburg, Pennsylvania and he also immortalized the phrase: "*Trust in God and fear nothing*".

In 1921, we moved to Bourbon, Mississippi in Washington County near Greenville, in the Mississippi River delta area. My Dad had been a subsistence farmer in Alabama and Uncle Ollie J. Rivers offered Poppa the opportunity to farm as a sharecropper in Mississippi, raising cotton on halves with the landowner. In the Delta, we were able to harvest as much as three bales of cotton per acre whereas in Alabama we only got one bale per acre. There were three brothers of the Rivers family related to us Griffins- Ollie, Jack, and Bealie. Uncle Ollie owned nine hundred acres of rich, black farmland known as pan dirt and he also had many Blacks living in "shotgun" houses and working on his farmland as sharecroppers. I remember that Uncle Ollie furnished the rural farm house that we lived in, all the seed, the mules, the farm implements and tools, and the land of which we worked at least eighty acres. We furnished all the labor and had no barn. The house we lived in was built on high log stilts and we'd drive the mules under the house and hang the harness on a peg under the floor. The terms of sharecropping were that we furnished all the labor to farm and gave up half of the income from the sale of the cotton harvest. Uncle Ollie owned the cotton gin and a tragic event happened during our Mississippi episode. Bealie Rivers was taking a farm wagon loaded with cotton to the gin and the mules got spooked and ran away. The wagon turned over and he was smothered to death under the overturned load and I remember seeing his body laid out on a bed for the funeral.

Poppa bought a milk cow in Leland and I had to walk this cow home, a distance of ten miles. My job was to lead our milk cow and stake her out on a ditch bank or in a grassy place so she could graze all day and then bring her home and water her. Momma milked the cow and I had to help churn the milk to get our butter and another of my jobs was to wash clothes on a scrub board. All during this time we used coal oil lamps at night. We had a lot of black dirt mud when it rained in the delta and I recall an experience in rural driving. Quill and I rode in Uncle Ollie's Model T Ford with four or five Walker hound dogs in the back seat. We slid off the road into a ditch and I had all the hound dogs piled on top of me. We pushed the T-Ford back onto the dirt road and went on our way. All of us children went to the Arcola School about fifteen miles away and two of my older brothers, Hellis and Quill, drove the only two school buses. I remember that I suffered a lot with the malaria fever and at times I had to be brought home from school with a high fever. I recall that I took a lot of quinine during this time.

During the time that we lived in the river delta of Mississippi, my parents attended the Southern Baptist Church in the small town of Bourbon, about twenty miles from Greenville. When I was about twelve years old, I did what was expected of many young American boys and girls; I formally joined the church. I remember when I got up out of my seat, walked down the aisle and the preacher met me out in front of the pulpit and shook my hand and congratulated me. That same Sunday afternoon, I rode on the running board of a Model T Ford to a big drainage ditch that had sufficient water in it. I was baptized by immersion and I rode back to town with my wet clothes on. That night during the church service, I was asked to stand in front of the pulpit and the whole congregation came up in a line to shake my hand and welcome me into the fellowship of the church. Now, I was officially a member of the Baptist Church. That was all I had to do to become a church member in good standing. I don't recall my father or mother or any of my brothers and sisters nor do I recall anyone else ever talking to me about inviting Jesus Christ into my life or having a personal relationship with the Lord. All I had ever heard was to get baptized and join the church and that would take care of everything. Soon after my ditch baptism and official church membership, our Griffin family prepared to move from the Mississippi Delta to Chicago, Illinois. Being an honest sharecropping Southern farmer wasn't easy and my Dad could not get along very well with my uncle Ollie Rivers. The move to Chicago from the delta area was something new and we never looked back as we traveled.

TWO

Chicago and the Winds of Change

About 1924, my Dad decided to move to Chicago, Illinois where my oldest sister Iree and her husband John Armistead had taken up residence. The bright lights of the big city attracted Iree and my brother-in-law had secured employment at the Link-Belt Manufacturing Company when jobs were scarce. They had invited us to come north to live and work in Chicago. Our first place of residence at 813 Marshfield Avenue was in a tough, West Chicago neighborhood. We moved around from one place to another in Chicago and I went to a different school each year. In 1932, I finished the eleventh grade in the town of Cicero, a suburb of Chicago.

All during the eight years that we lived in that big city, I don't remember any of my family regularly attending any church. I didn't know the Lord Jesus Christ and made no profession of faith. I was in the world and of the world, running around with the crowd, doing what the rest of the crowd was doing. I didn't go to any church, I didn't read the Bible and I certainly didn't claim to be a Christian. About the only kind of churches I had heard of were the Baptist and Methodist and I really didn't have any substantial theological knowledge of either. As far as any of the family or I knew at that time, our ancestors had all been Baptists so in our minds, we were more or less carrying on a family tradition. The ceremony of baptism and the act of joining a local Baptist church had no real effect on my life. Nothing in my being had changed spiritually or morally. As I continued to grow up, I followed the worldly crowd, especially during the time we lived in Chicago. I ran with a local street gang and was arrested on one occasion for stealing a bicycle chain but didn't have to spend any time in jail due to the mercifulness of the presiding judge. My Dad would pray beside his bed in the evenings and lead in prayer at the table at mealtime but he never approached me in a personal manner about prayer for my eternal soul. I want to clearly say that based on Biblical and sociological evidences, my family and friends apparently knew nothing about true Christianity. Truthfully, it appears that all that they ever knew or practiced was a form of religion that could be called "Church-anity". Jesus said: "*I thank thee, O Father, Lord of heaven and earth, because thou hast hid these things from the wise and prudent* (proud and sophisticated), *and hast revealed them unto babes* (humble and un-educated). *Even so, Father: for so it seemed good in thy sight*". (Matthew 11:25, 26)

The time we lived in Chicago and in Cicero was during the "roaring twenties" when Al Capone and other gangsters were in the height of their careers in crime. I can remember very well the crime wars that they fought openly in our city streets during Prohibition. More than once, there would be a shootout on the west side area of Chicago. Several times, a few of the gangsters would round up some of the neighborhood children and buy them ice cream cones at the corner drugstore that had a soda fountain. Al Capone was finally caught and convicted and sent away to Alcatraz Prison off the coast of California. One winter while we were living on Washtaunau Street in the suburb of Cicero, I could hardly wait for a pond that was across the railroad tracks to freeze completely over so we could go ice-skating. One afternoon, I decided to add a little more excitement to the sport by driving my Dad's Model T Ford out onto the frozen pond in order to slide around on the ice in an automobile. A buddy of mine and I were in the front seat when we drove out on the frozen pond. As we neared the center of the pond, I could hear the popping and snapping of the ice as it began breaking up. I knew what that meant so I hollered for my friend to run for it. I jumped out and ran slipping and sliding to the left and my friend scrambled to the right and we both managed to reach the shore without getting our feet wet. The ice was broken up in big chunks and the Model T sank to the bottom with about two inches of the roof sticking out of the cold water. I went to my maternal Uncle Quincy Keel who was my confidential friend and he hired two tow trucks to pull the car out of the pond. They cleaned it out, and changed the oils in the motor, transmission and differential. I took the car home and parked it in the garage. If my Dad had of found out about the incident, I would have gotten a whipping that I would have never forgotten.

In about 1929, Hellis and Quill bought a four-cylinder, Ford Model A Roadster with a rumble seat in the back. The open-air rumble seat was designed with a trunk lid with a backrest on the inside and it would accommodate luggage or could seat two people. This vehicle was stolen and when the police found the car, it had been completely stripped. I recall in 1929, when the great depression hit the United States. We had always been a poor family, but now we really felt the economic pinch. Our family continued living in the Cicero area and in 1931, I was enrolled in the eleventh grade at the J. Sterling Morton High School about a mile from where we lived. The winter temperatures would sometimes drop to zero degrees or lower and in spite of the cold, my sister and I would have to walk to school. On account of the great number of students enrolled, the school had two shifts and my shift started at 6:00 A.M. I got out of school at 12:00 noon at which time the afternoon shift began and it ended at 6:00 P.M. I enjoyed going to school there due to the machine shop class and for the harmonica class where I learned to play the mouth harp. The harmonica class had about forty members with several kinds of instruments, some were bass and some were chromatics. At that time we had the genuine Hohner harmonicas, which were made only in Germany and imported to the United States. We could buy a new Hohner harmonica in Chicago for fifty cents. For many years I played worldly tunes but later, when I was saved, I began to play only Gospel music. At the present time a new Hohner harmonica costs around thirty dollars and the option is to buy one made in China for around seven dollars but they don't last near as long.

Somehow, we made it to the year of 1932, when after working at the Fair Store in downtown Chicago for about seven years; my Dad lost his job as a shoe salesman. My Dad's sister Ida Griffin Harrison and her husband Uncle Hard Harrison lived in Levy County, Florida and my Dad kept in touch with them. He decided to move from Chicago to Florida and we made preparations for the big move back to the Deep South. I was only seventeen years old and I was the only one available to drive "Pop's" black, two-door, 1925, Model T Ford to Florida. My brother Hellis put me behind the steering wheel and had me to drive around the block a few times as my crash course for driver's education.

We left for Florida the next day traveling in two cars. Hellis drove his dark blue, four-door, 1929, Model M Hupmobile sedan with a powerful straight-line, eight-cylinder engine. Riding with Hellis in the front seat were Poppa. In the back seat were Meldee, Dell and Byrd. They also carried luggage inside and on top of the car. I drove the Model T Ford and riding with me were Momma and Kate and we hauled our bedding. While passing through Tennessee, we drove the route over Lookout Mountain near Chattanooga. Starting down the mountain, I thought I would save some gasoline by shutting off the engine and coasting downhill for a ways. The car got to going faster and faster and I pushed one pedal after another until the brakes and transmission bands burned out. Finally, I got the engine running again and used the gears and motor to slow the car down and we made it safely to the bottom of Lookout Mountain where Hellis and the rest of the family were waiting. We had to re-line the transmission bands and then continued on our way to Florida without any further mishaps.

THREE

Levy County in Dixie Land

"Pop" went back to farming as soon as we arrived in Chiefland, Florida and found a place to live. In 1933, Pop rented about eighty acres of land from Mr. Usher on the Cedar Keys Road. I started back to school and in May 1933, graduated from the twelfth grade at Chiefland High School. The school buses didn't run during my last year in high school and getting to school in my senior year was difficult. I had to carry my lunch in an old lard bucket. My Dad didn't have the money to buy a graduation ring for me and my brother-in-law gave me a suit of clothes to wear to the graduation ceremony. I was determined to finish school whatever the cost and I graduated from high school in spite of the times and trials! Eventually, Pop bought eighty acres from Mr. Henry Durrance on the Manatee Springs Road a few miles out from Chiefland. Dad sold an acre to a man fronting the road so that he could build a house to live in. In time, about sixty acres of this property was under cultivation. The rest of the land was un-cleared wood and palmetto thickets where wild hogs roamed and rattlesnakes slithered. We cut pine trees from the wooded area for stove wood. We had two mules and the implements to work the land. The family members provided the labor and I don't recall Pop ever hiring any farm hands.

After I graduated, I decided that farming was not for me. As long as I can remember, I had been fascinated with steam locomotives.

Now, the opportunity came for me to experience trains from a closer perspective. Just after graduation, a cousin named Clyde Harrison wanted to see the World's Fair in Chicago so he and I discussed making this trip a reality. We made up our minds to make the trip as hoboes and we told no one of our plans, not even my Mother. The Atlantic Coastline Railroad came through Chiefland and we knew that it stopped in town about 10:00 o'clock at night to take on a load of fish brought from the nearby Gulf of Mexico. On the night we were ready to leave, we each had a bag packed and we stopped to visit my girl friend that lived near where the train stopped. When we heard the train whistle blow, we left her home, retrieved our bags and walked down to where the train was stopped, taking on water for the engine. We climbed up on the water tank and found several other hoboes already sitting around. Clyde and I positioned ourselves on the top of the train and we rode through the night, putting up with the coal dust and cinders hitting us in the face. At 8:00 o'clock the next morning, we arrived in Montgomery, Alabama and spent the day with Clyde's mother. That afternoon, we caught another train northward. We rode four different railroad systems and slept little. I believe it was near Cincinnati, Ohio that we weren't having too much success in trying to catch a freight train that was already going too fast and we were running as fast as we could. The flagman saw we couldn't make it aboard so he pulled the signal cord and the train slowed down allowing us to catch the caboose. We climbed the stairs and went into the caboose and the flagman gave us some sandwiches and ice water. We rode on freight trains for three days and nights.

When we finally arrived in Chicago, we were black being covered with coal dust and soot. We got to see the World's Fair held in Chicago from May 27th to November 1, 1933, located adjacent to the railroad station and yards. The theme of the World's Fair was: "1833-1933, A Century of Progress", but I noticed that segregation was in effect there just as much as in the South. African-Americans had a separate designated day in which to attend the fair. We stayed with my brother-in-law John Armistead and his brother Roy and we worked with John hanging wallpaper. In spite of the Constitutional Prohibition on beer and liquor, Roy would obtain hops and barley and made homebrewed beer in a couple of large 10 to 15-gallon clay or ceramic crocks in a dark closet in their apartment. Clyde and I were called upon to help bottle up the brew and we put a teaspoon of sugar in each bottle before capping. In return, Roy let Clyde and I drive his Willis car around town to hang out with our friends. We were a couple of Florida boys in the big city, free as a breeze and on a roll. I was gone from home for about nine months and finally decided to dangerously hobo alone on the trains back to Florida. For an entire night, I rode on top of a boxcar lying down on the walkway. I lay on the planks with my head on my arms as I grasped the edges of the walkway. I would drop off to sleep and wake up at short intervals to find myself still holding on. On the return trip, I stopped over in Clarksburg, Mississippi to visit with my uncle Bunyan Keel and his wife Virginia. I walked into their home just as they were having breakfast. I always admired Uncle Bunyan and Aunt Virginia.

I was riding on top of another boxcar in a different freight train when I finally arrived about three-o-clock one afternoon in the little town of Chiefland, Florida. My brother Byrd and sisters Kate and Dell were just getting out of school and I got to the town in time to catch the school bus with them and we rode the seven miles out of town to the Griffin home and farm. My mother had worried about me all the time I was gone from home and she must have had a premonition that I was coming back. When the school bus stopped in front of the gate, my mother was standing on the front porch, looking toward the road, her hands in her apron. I think she saw me before I got out of the bus and I didn't stop to open the gate, I jumped over it and ran to take my mother in my arms. I had been gone for nine months and now was safe back at home with my family.

Even after we had moved down to Florida, the great depression was still on and somehow my Dad made a go of farming the sandy, loamy soil in Levy County. We grew crops such as corn, peanuts, watermelons and the green variety of sugar cane. All of us worked in harvesting the cane and hauling it to be piled near the mill. It was my job to get up before daylight, hitch the mules and turn the cane mill in order to squeeze a barrel of fresh cane juice before Pop got up. Then he would strain and pour the juice into a sixty-gallon iron cauldron, light a fire under it and cook the syrup into cane molasses. He would stir the boiling juice as it thickened and his skill acquired through experience would determine the right consistency of the sweet molasses and the precise moment to rake the fire out from under the cauldron. In addition to homemade cane syrup, we had boiled peanuts, sweet corn, a variety of home-grown vegetables, and watermelon in season. Pop divided his cultivated land into twenty or forty-acre parcels and grew different crops in each parcel.

Hellis worked a great deal with Pop in the farming and one time lost his wallet containing some cash money while plowing in the field with the mules. He recovered his lost wallet and money the following season while plowing the same field. He took the money to the bank and they exchanged his rotten notes for new bills. I always have had a great deal of admiration and respect for Hellis because he worked very hard to help support our whole family. We had a milk cow or two in one pasture or another and also quite a few chickens running loose on the yard and we would have to look around for the eggs. We depended for much of our groceries from the farming and large family garden. We would harvest our own field corn and store it in the corncrib and from this family resource, feed the mules and also shell and grind our own corn meal to feed ourselves. Our hogs usually ran loose in a fenced portion of our property known as the palmetto thickets and woods and a portion of our peanut crop was used to fatten the hogs in order to sell them on the market. We also slaughtered about nine hogs a year during the crisp fall and winter season when it was cooler weather. We had our own smokehouse where hams, bacon, mullet fish and sausage would cure and be available for our use during the winter and into the spring and summer months. It was a treat to make and eat chitlins and cracklings. I recall that we would frequently plow up arrowheads and flint scrapers in the fields. Deep in the wooded area of Pop's land, there was an old limestone sinkhole that the Indians had lived around during ancient times until early pioneering days. One of my young friends from Hardee Town was Cecil who would sometimes steal a carton of Camel cigarettes from his Dad's store and we would smoke every one of them, filter less and full bore.

After the hobo trip by train to Chicago, I worked a while on the WPA and then in November or December of 1933, I joined a Civilian Conservation Corps Camp in Florida. This was a work program instituted in 1932, by President- Franklin Delano Roosevelt. We were sent to Fort Barrancas at Pensacola for CCC training, then sent to West Bay to start our work of building bridges, constructing dirt roads, planting trees, putting up telephone lines, plowing fire lanes, building fire lookout towers, fighting forest fires and doing forestry work in general. Our CCC Camp was Company #1416, located on Holmes Creek between Chipley and Bonifay, Florida and I stayed in the CCC for two years to learn the skills of surveying and drawing maps. It was a great experience for me to work in the outdoors and to manage a work crew consisting of as many as eight men. I rose to the position of crew leader by the end of my stay in the CCC and enjoyed the responsibility of being in charge of a barrack of fifty men. Being in the CCC camp was an experience I will never forget. Neither will I forget our President- Mr. Franklin Delano Roosevelt, who made it possible. This was one president that I along with many other Americans deeply appreciated, loved and respected. As it turned out, I served one hitch in the CCC, 1933, to 1935. Mr. Roosevelt was the only president ever elected to serve in office for the fourth term.

The CCC camp was almost like being in the Army. We had a US Army captain over us and we were taught cleanliness and strict discipline and on Saturday mornings, we would have a thorough inspection. One of our officers would come into our barracks with a pair of white gloves on and run his fingers over the tops of the doors and the windows. If there was a coating of dust and his gloves were soiled, there would be no Saturday night passes to town. Not being able to go to town on Saturday night was an almost unbearable fate. It didn't happen many times. I recall one Saturday night, one of my buddies who was bad to drink had gotten pretty saturated and he was riding in the passenger side of the car. He had drunk too much, got sick on his stomach and when he leaned out the window to throw up; his head hit a rural mailbox. He survived the incident after a brush with death and getting about 18 stitches. This accident sobered us up to some extent for a while. The work experience and job skills that I acquired in the CCC came in handy later on in my life. This was a part of God's plan for my life and ministry.

I left the CCC in 1935, and found work in making maps for a small company. These maps had to be hand drawn with ditto ink and special drawing instruments. I moved around for a while and in the spring of 1936, ended up in Live Oak, Florida. The nature of my map work made it necessary to access data from record books archived at the City Halls and the County Court Houses of the area. I was in the Live Oak area for a month or more and for lunch one day, I went into the Blue Wing Café where they served home style Southern cuisine. After being seated, I looked up to see the waitress coming to take my order and it was hard for me to take my eyes off her. She was very pretty and it just happened that at the time, I was seriously looking for a wife. I was now twenty years old and had asked a girl in my hometown to marry me but she told me she wanted to finish her career. She was a blonde anyway and I really preferred brunettes. The waitress in the Blue Wing Café was a brown-haired girl and her name was Anna Adele Roberts. Of course I asked her for a date but she played hard to get.

The Roberts family came from a French Huguenot ancestry. The Rev. Pierre Robert and his family had emigrated in 1686, from Switzerland to Charleston, South Carolina. He was a pastor in the French Santee colony. A member of this family, Lewis Roberts, participated in the American Revolution under General Francis Marion known as the "Swamp Fox" in South Carolina. After the revolution, the surname was anglicized to Roberts and some members of this family tree spread out into the wiregrass region of Southeast Georgia and by the 1840's, into Columbia County in north Florida. By the time of the War Between the States, Adele's grandparents; Reubin and Harriett Johns Roberts had become settled in Suwannee County, Florida. For many years Adele's parents had farmed in the O'Brien community just south of Live Oak not far from the Suwannee River. The Live Oak and Perry and Gulf Rail Road passed through both communities in Suwannee County. This route was part of an old logging road built by Thomas Dowling in the late 1880's and the railroad was known locally as the famous "Loping Gopher." For some of its distance, it ran parallel to Highway #129 which was known at the time as Dixie Highway.

The next time I visited the Blue Wing Café, Adele said she would go on a date with me and we went to the movies. From then on, we went out to the dance halls pretty often and we enjoyed dancing and drinking beer, wine and whiskey chased with Coca-Cola all night. We both smoked cigarettes and drank liquor and I found out later that when Adele was twelve years old, she had become a member of the Baptist church in the same customary manner that I had. When she was a young girl, she was baptized and had joined the Baptist church and in reality, neither one of us knew anything about being a Born-Again Christian. During the time of our youth, no one had given us a copy of the Bible and no one had ever really tried to present the Lord Jesus Christ to either of us. I consider this oft repeated scenario to be a great tragedy here in America. It wasn't until I enlisted in the US Army Air Force that I was issued a copy of the New Testament. There is a great gulf of difference between mere religion and true Christianity. Many people believe that variations of the religious ceremony of water baptism play a critical part in salvation but this is erroneous. The denominational persuasion that water baptism provides salvation is a false theological concept. The ritual of water baptism does not regenerate any sinner and it is only by the shed blood of Jesus Christ that we are made whole by Grace through Faith.

FOUR

The Griffin Family

After Adele and I had been dating for about a month and a half, I asked her to marry me. I think she was as willing to get married as I was so I asked her to set the date, which was August 1, 1936. Adele talked with her oldest sister; Mrs. Verde Roberts Bullock about having the wedding ceremony in her home in Monticello, Florida and it was agreed upon. I paid five dollars for the marriage license, five dollars for the ring and I paid Pastor- R. B. Mayfield of the First Baptist Church, five dollars for officiating the ceremony. We had not informed any of our family about our wedding except for Bill and Verde Roberts Bullock in Monticello. After the wedding, we went to visit with Adele's widowed mother Anna Francis Baden Roberts living on her farm near Adele's hometown of O'Brien in Suwannee County. This was near the Suwannee River.

Afterwards, on our way to Jacksonville, we stopped over at Madison to spend a night in a motel. We rented an apartment in Jacksonville and I went to work with the Florida State Planning Board. I worked as a topographical map draftsman with Mr. Elmore who had been my engineer in the CCC at Chipley, Florida. I had acquired this skill in the CCC and would use the skill later on in the US Army Air Force. During our stay in Jacksonville, my sister Kate came and stayed with us for a while so she could attend the Massey Business College. My brother-in-law, John Armistead who at this time was working on a boat bringing bananas from Cuba to Florida, would visit us and bring bananas. Adele and I would have our ups and downs, we'd have a fuss or a fight over something of no great consequence and then make up and how sweet that would be. We never went to any church except for a marriage or a funeral. We didn't have a Bible and we didn't take the time to read one or go to church. We both claimed to be Baptists but were ignorant of the Bible and according to the world's standard; we were strictly in the world and of the world.

After we had lived in Jacksonville for about six months, the opportunity for me to earn more money presented itself and I began working for the Florida Forest Service as a Forestry Technician. We then moved to the community of Foley near Perry, Florida where we lived for less than a year.

I remember that the working conditions required a great deal of walking in wooded areas in order to make surveys of the different types of standing timber and maps of the general topography. There were plenty of poisonous snakes and alligators in the palmetto thickets, ponds, woods and swamps we had to traverse almost daily. I had a crew of six to eight men and we had a stake body truck for our transportation. We were very fortunate that no one in our crew ever got snake bit or attacked by a Florida gator. Generally, we spotted or heard the snakes and killed them first. At times the wild hogs would eat the snakes. At times during the winter, there would be a skim of ice on the ponds and when we arrived on the scene in the frosty mornings, some of the men would jump in and break the ice and then be ready to go to work.

Some time in 1937, Adele and I moved back to Chiefland and we entered into a partnership with Hellis Griffin, my oldest brother. We rented the Rite-Way Filling Station located across the road from the Chiefland High School. Adele and I lived in the back part of the full-service gasoline station and the three of us operated this business sixteen hours a day, seven days a week. We didn't have time to read the Bible or go to church. At this time, Adele and I made no claim of being Christians although my oldest brother did. We sold beer, soda pop, tobacco products, some groceries, gasoline and other petroleum products, performed light mechanical work, and also fixed flat tires.

We carried brand name merchandise and the quality of our customer service extended from the counter to the curb. In the establishment, we had pinball machines and gambling devices. Just about all gas stations and stores had gambling devices or punchboards and we earned a thirty percent profit off these popular gambling devices. We also had a music jukebox which played records at five-cents a song. Almost all candies, sodas, ice cream, and snacks cost a nickel. We were there to make as much money as we could. Adele and I managed very well and by the fall of 1938, we purchased a brand-new, black, two-door sedan 1939, Chevrolet with white-wall tires. We made a down payment and then finished paying it off ahead of time and we got a rebate.

We sold fireworks on Christmas the same as the fourth of July and we would shoot off fireworks around the station until the ground would be covered with bits of paper. We became popular and well liked in the community and business was very good. The Bible says: "*If you were of the world, the world would love its own*". (John 15:19) Our first child, Johnny was born in the spring of 1939 and Dr. Cammack spent the night in our home in order to attend the birth. We had purchased a house with two acres and water well on the Manatee Springs Road from John Armistead for $500.00. We continued to do very well in business and when the 1941 models of automobiles came out, we bought our second new car, a 1941, Chevrolet deluxe sedan.

I remember when we did get a few hours off from the gas station, we'd go up to the Black Diamond, leave Johnny Ray asleep on the back seat of the car and dance, smoke and drink with the juke joint crowd until the wee hours of the morning. We'd always lose sleep because after all night at the juke joints, we'd have to go back to work at the gas station the next day. This was what the rest of the crowd was doing. Some of the crowd went to church and some didn't. We had to take turns going to the ball games and arguments would arise about whose turn it was to go to see a ball game. I especially liked going to the girl's basketball games. Adele also liked these games since she had played basketball in high school at O'Brien.

It was about the first part of 1941, that we left the gas station business and I went to work with the Florida Forest Service as a Forest ranger. They furnished me with a pick-up truck with a radio and I had the supervisory responsibility of all of Levy County, Florida including four steel lookout towers. I had to maintain about two hundred miles of telephone cable connecting the lookout towers. Adele and I had squabbles all along because we were carnal and not spiritual. As a result of the Japanese bombing of Pearl Harbor in Hawaii, the United States declared war on Japan on December 8, 1941, quickly followed by a declaration of war on Germany made on December 11, 1941. Our government began to ration almost everything in order to have sufficient resources to use in the war effort. While we were dancing one night at the Nightingale Dance Hall near the town of Gainesville, Florida someone stole a tire off our car. I got quite angry over the incident especially since tires were being rationed and new automobile tires were really difficult to get.

FIVE

World War II

A diplomatic consensus was reached by Mr. Chamberlain and Herr Hitler. The famous declaration made to the world that there was to be: "Peace in our time", proved to be very short lived. Most Americans including myself were very upset about the "Day of Infamy" as President Franklin Delano Roosevelt called the Japanese attack on Pearl Harbor. It soon became clear that the war that was brewing was to be on two fronts and would involve and impact the world. We knew that Uncle Sam needed our help and I began to talk with the boys around Chiefland about volunteering in the Army Air Force and getting the war over with. Several of my acquaintances were ready to go and seventeen of us young men volunteered for military duty. I enlisted and took the oath on November 3, 1942, from Levy County, Florida into military service at Camp Blanding.

We became soldiers in the "AC" or Army Air Corps and were completely at our country's service. We were promised several concessions such as being able to live off post if married, no Kitchen Police duty, no overseas assignments and we were offered our choice of airfields to be stationed at. We chose Tyndale Field at Panama City, Florida on the coast of the Gulf of Mexico. We understood that we were to become trained aircraft mechanics and we were to have a permanent assignment at this field. When the "Brass" found out that I was a topographic map draftsman, they re-assigned me to the drafting department # 070 in the Army Air Force. I was assigned to Headquarter 331 Station Compliment Squadron APO 652 and went from Private to Corporal in short order. My brother Byrd, being ten years younger than I, was chosen to go to gunnery school to be trained as an aerial gunner on a B-24 Liberator bomber. He was soon sent to England and began to make daylight-bombing missions over Europe and Germany. The bomber he flew in was named Gator. Adele and I remained at Panama City for another year and a half. Of the entire group who enlisted from Chiefland, only Byrd and I went overseas.

While on a three-day leave, my name was selected for over seas shipment. Upon returning to base from leave, the process began for me to ship out as soon as possible. I was sent to Greensboro, North Carolina and Adele and I drove our car and carried Johnny Ray with us. I stayed at Greensboro for about two weeks and then was sent on to Boston, Massachusetts on a troop train. On June 27, 1944, we unloaded directly from the train onto the converted troop ship, the Mauritania. This enormous, 800 foot long ship had been a British luxury liner before the war and was now impressed into duty as a maritime troop carrier. I enjoyed my trip across the Atlantic on this great ship. We set sail from Boston, Massachusetts with several thousand men on board headed for the war in Europe. We were loaded aboard in alphabetical order and being enlisted men, we were placed in compartments below the water line. In case of a German submarine attack, the torpedo would penetrate the ship's hull in the event of a direct hit. For this reason, the commissioned officers were given quarters above the water line. This gave the officers a better chance to survive a torpedo attack than we enlisted men. I didn't know it then but it was reported later that the route we took across the Northern Atlantic was known as submarine alley. It was there that more of our Allied ships were sunk in World War Two than anywhere else in the world. On more than one occasion, we could feel the shaking of the ship when depth charges were rolled off the stern and exploded in the water below us.

We only had two meals per day and I really liked the fish and chips. Being that we were accommodated alphabetically, most of the men's names in my compartment started with the letter G. Well, there were four of us from this compartment that banded together to make our rounds doing chores aboard the ship. We were known as the "Four G's". We would take turns standing in line to fill our canteens with drinking water and to buy a candy bar at the ship's Canteen. We soon discovered that there were orderlies that would line up at the mess in order to get trays of food to take up to the officer's quarters. We put two and two together and decided to get better chow by standing in this line and upon getting the tray, instead of going up, we'd go down and find a place to eat our catch.

Taking a bath was pretty rough because we had to bathe in salt water. We must have run into a bad storm or a hurricane due to our running in some heavy seas for about three days. The ship traveled fast enough so that we were un-escorted all the way across the North Atlantic to England. We were six days and six night's crossing over the ocean and we finally sailed down between Ireland and England and we docked at Liverpool, England in the United Kingdom on July 5, 1944. We disembarked onto a train to Bath, England, and then we were trucked out to a military camp in a cow pasture. Our trip from Boston to Bath was a good trip and someday, I'd like to take another such voyage as a soldier in the ministry for the Lord Jesus Christ.

Riding on that English train to Bath, England was a unique experience. We sat in seats facing each other and saw some of the countryside. At Bath, we lived in pyramidal tents and the camp had a decent field kitchen. My assigned task was to erect field tents for more incoming soldiers and to dig latrines. I did pretty well on field-cooked rations. I found out that my brother Byrd was stationed in northern England and had finished his thirty bombing missions over Europe on D-Day, June 6, 1944. I had to wait in line for almost three hours in order to talk with him on a phone and in the excitement of talking with him; I risked a court martial for having given him the specific location of my outfit. He managed to get a weeklong pass and he rode the train about 400 miles down to where I was located. I was standing in front of my tent, # 17 when my brother came riding up in an army jeep. I crawled across the hood to grab him and hug his neck. I loved my younger brother and felt a responsibility for his well-being and as a sinner; I didn't know how to pray for him, I just sweated the time away in my concern for him. I knew enough about the European bombing missions by now to realize that he had been through a living hell if that is possible. I let him sleep in my bed that night which was not the steam-heated barracks he was accustomed to living in. The next morning, he had a bad case of strep throat and the doctor put him to bed rest in the camp hospital for nearly a week. On the last day of his leave, we got a pass and went into the town of Bath to do some sightseeing. We saw an old Roman bathing pool that still had hot running water from thermal springs and the next day, he took the train back to his airbase.

After several days, the entire HQ 331st Station Compliment Squadron was shipped out to France. Our military outfit was a replacement depot and had about two hundred men, three or four Military Police and one or two Sergeants. We crossed the English Channel on a naval vessel and we had to go over the side of the ship with a full pack to climb down the side of the ship on a large rope ladder into a smaller landing craft called the Higgins Boat. We waded ashore from the landing craft onto and across Omaha Beach where the bloody D-Day invasion of France had recently taken place. When we climbed the hill behind the beach, we could see the new cemetery where about three thousand of our American soldiers, casualties of the D-Day invasion, had just been buried. For the first time, my heart sank and I fully realized that this war was for keeps. We marched about five miles inland to a cow pasture. We had to put up our pup tents in the darkness and had just climbed in and stretched out to relax when it seemed the whole world came to an end. The whole sky lit up like at noonday. It sounded like the sky was being ripped apart and everybody was running around looking for a hole or trench to get into. When I found a hole, someone was already in it. Then, just as suddenly as it began, it was over. Some of our own anti-aircraft guns in the immediate vicinity had begun firing on an enemy plane and the scare was on us. The next morning, we were loaded aboard army trucks and carried further inland to another cow pasture and set up camp with pyramidal tents and a field kitchen. It seemed that no one knew what we were supposed to do.

After a few weeks of wading around in the mud, we broke camp, loaded our gear onto army trucks and we were carried to Paris. Apparently, it was a bit premature for us to be there since some fighting with the Germans was still going on in the suburbs of Paris and our outfit was carried back to camp out in the area of the Normandy landing. At one point, some men of our HQ 331st Station Complement Squadron visited Saint Marie Eglise and later in August or September, some of us went over to the coast to visit the historic old monastery of Mont Saint Michelle. The ground floor level had shops with postcards and souvenirs and the stone stair steps leading up to the higher levels were rounded from the centuries of use. A Catholic Church sanctuary was at the very top and the German Army had used Mont Saint Michelle as a radio communication station during their occupation of France.

In a few more weeks, we were carried back to Paris and we were situated in a French chateau called the House of Rothschild. This large building had a fireplace in every room but there was no coal and very little else to burn for heat. We had to wear our winter uniform and overcoats all the time. I wore my long-john or thermal underwear for a whole month and there was no way to bathe for as long a time. The drinking water was contaminated so we drank all the cognac we could get. I had a close buddy from Alabama and since I was already thirty years old, the fellows in my unit called me "Old Man". Our unit was part of the Ninth US Army Air Force in France and our job was to process replacement GI's being sent to the front lines and other soldiers returning to the rear for whatever reasons. My spec number 070 meant that I was specially qualified in cartography. No topographical maps were needed at the time I was in Paris and the alternative job for me was as assistant Military Postmaster. We processed many types of mail, parcels and Christmas packages. Mail call was held every afternoon at four o'clock and 200 or more American soldiers would gather to receive correspondence from home. In spite of American officer's having a priority on liquor allotments from stateside ahead of the enlisted men's mail call, they would sometimes share drinks with the enlisted men. I recall that we processed bags of mail that had been retrieved from the ocean. Many ships were sunk by German submarines and it was critically important that floating mail bags be kept from falling into enemy hands. We found that many letters were water soaked and packages were deteriorated and the contents falling out.

While we were in France, we didn't go lacking for cigarettes. Included in the K-Rations would generally be a small pack of three cigarettes, which were furnished by the US Government. Then, on top of that we could buy the top line of cigarettes for fifty-cents a carton or five-cents a pack. I smoked more cigarettes while overseas as most everyone else due to the stress and tension but this habit was very detrimental to my health. American military personnel could buy cigarettes cheap and we would take the smokes to perfume shops and barter those for bottles of the famous Channel Number Five perfume to send back home. I did this several times for Adele and my sisters. I was invited to eat supper one evening with a French family in Paris. They served cooked greens, sliced French bread, boiled eggs, and a glass of wine. The French cuisine was very different from our US Army rations.

For some reason, my teeth began to get loose and it was hard for me to chew any food. The drinking water was polluted and a lot of chlorine was added which made me sick on my stomach. No one paid attention to me in spite of the fact that I was sick much of the time. The K-rations had chemical preservatives and enhancers in them and they hurt my stomach. I had told the examining military physicians when I enlisted that I had a weak stomach but they paid little attention. I had been told that I would not be assigned overseas. I suffered from a sour stomach; cramps, acid reflux and I couldn't hold the K-Rations down. I slept on the top bunk and during the nights, I'd grind my teeth to the extent that the Postmaster sleeping in the bottom bunk would wake up swearing and kick the top bunk to make me stop. It was during this time that we were issued K-rations and my health went from bad to worse. I toughed it out for about five months before I gave it up and went on sick call.

The cold winter of 1944, was also bad to worse in our front lines. On December 15, 1944, the Germans made a break through known as the Battle of the Bulge. The Germans dropped paratroopers around the city of Paris dressed in American G.I. uniforms and there were German Army snipers killing our soldiers. The American Army was taken by surprise and needed more men at once. Consequently, men were taken from any where in the military they could be found. My name was posted on the bulletin board to go up to the front. It was during the time that I was stationed in Paris, France that President Franklin Delano Roosevelt died. When the American soldiers heard of his death, many combat hardened soldiers wept openly over the loss of our beloved leader.

My teeth were in such bad condition; I could almost pull them out with my fingers. I had an appointment with the army dentist and when he looked at me, he told me in no uncertain tones, "I'll have to pull all your teeth out." I put up an argument but it was to no avail. I was put into the base hospital and the next morning, the army dentist pulled eight teeth from my top gum. Three days later, he pulled the other eight top teeth. It was a bloody and painful ordeal and my face swelled up almost the size of a football so they gave me penicillin. Later, the dentist pulled some of the teeth from the bottom gum and now I couldn't chew at all and was being given all liquids to eat. I was now at the 203rd General Hospital in Paris, France. A French girl I had met insisted on coming back to America with me even after I explained that I was married. She visited me in the 203rd General Hospital and after seeing me with half of my teeth gone, excused herself and she never returned. After several days in the hospital, the doctors began making x-rays of my stomach and digestive tract. Everything seemed to move along quite slowly and when the x-rays were developed and examined, the attending doctor came to my bed and told me to get all my clothes and things together and that I'd be going to the United Kingdom.

There were several soldiers in my group that were being sent back to England for further medical attention and we were carried to Le Bourget Airfield, the same airfield where Charles A. Lindberg had landed upon arriving in France after his solo, trans-Atlantic flight from New York in 1927. This causes me to digress for a moment in time. Upon returning to America, Charles Lindberg was an international hero. We were living in Chicago at that time and I took my mother on the L-train down to the loop to see the Lindberg welcome parade on Michigan Boulevard. I recall we could hear the band playing and we felt the pushing and shoving of the huge crowd. We never got to see Mr. Lindberg in the parade since my mother was of short stature and I was only thirteen years old and we couldn't see over the people's heads. The sidewalk was jam-packed from the curb to the buildings with the throng of people. We heard Mr. Lindberg's motorcade procession pass by and it seemed that everyone tried to leave at the same time. This was impossible and many people were being trampled, crushed, and plate-glass windows in the storefronts were being broken in from the pressure of the crowd. It took all my strength to protect my mother from being crushed and it is a miracle she wasn't suffocated. It seemed to take an hour to just get to the street corner and when we rounded that corner, the pressure of the mob rapidly decreased. I have been reluctant to get in a crowd like that ever since.

On April 14, 1945, several other sick soldiers and I were flown from Le Bourget airfield across the English Channel in a C-46 hospital plane and I was admitted to another hospital in southern England. I had a talk with the doctor after a day or two and they didn't give me any treatments. I was told that I would be returning to America and after about a week, I was loaded aboard a naval hospital ship and we set sail from South Hampton for the United States on April 21, 1945. I had volunteered to fight for my country and came very close to being in combat in the terrible winter of 1944, in France. I believe with all my heart that God spared my life in spite of losing all my teeth and having stomach problems. The Lord had plans for my life as a Missionary Evangelist and I give Him all the praise. There were about forty ships in the convoy and we stayed pretty close together for the duration of the voyage home since the war was still on and German U-boats were still prowling the Atlantic. It took fourteen days to cross the Atlantic and we landed at New York, City on Victory in Europe Day, May 5, 1945, and I was able to go and visit Times Square and see the crowd celebrating. We were given a free seven-minute telephone call to our families and I talked $10.00 over the time limit. We only stayed in New York City for about three days and we were sent on to Thomasville, Georgia where Adele and my mother came to meet me.

While I was at Thomasville, some false teeth were made for me. I had gained fourteen pounds, or a pound per day from all the good food we had been served on the hospital ship. I was doing much better by this time but the army wanted to keep me a little longer and I was sent to Miami Beach, Florida for another three months of rest and recuperation. My length of continental service was two years and seven days while my foreign service in the battles and campaigns of Northern France was ten months and nine days. I was awarded the decorations of the European Theater Operation Ribbon, Good Conduct Medal, and a Bronze Service Star with no time lost under AW 107 and issued a lapel button. I had volunteered for military duty and the outcome was very different from my initial perspective. Adele was able to come down to Miami and we stayed together until I was discharged on September 19, 1945, with a service-connected disability of forty-per-cent. My honorable discharge from the military came after Victory in Europe Day, May 8, 1945 and Victory in Japan Day on August 15, 1945. We had our own car with us and we drove straight home to Chiefland, Florida. The Second World War, the largest and most violent armed conflict in world history, was really over.

SIX

Jack R. Griffin, Service Station
— *Veteran* —

I had made a few attempts to pray at times during my military experience overseas, but the main theme of my "prayers" was for God to let me go home. That was all I wanted and all I could ask God for. God was indeed merciful to me and now I was back at home, free to do as I chose. I had made some business plans while I was in England and now that I was back at home, I wanted to go into a serious commercial venture for myself.

Soon after hearing that the Postmaster position in Chiefland would become available through the retirement of Mr. L. L. Calloway, I took the civil service exam and scored number two. Mr. Clarence Nettles had been Assistant Postmaster for several years and he scored number one on the exam. He was promoted to Postmaster and remained as such for many years. I had considered having a gasoline service station of my own and since my civilian occupation was as an auto mechanic, I decided to pursue this course of business. Initially, my younger brother Ivy B. Griffin and I wanted to be partners and he helped me start the construction of the building but a long term business association did not materialize. Adele and I had saved up some money, sold our car for $800.00 and with the additional help of the servicemen's provision of $100.00 a month for job training under the GI Bill, Adele and I bought building materials and

I went to work. Along with some hired help, it took me three months to build a block structure suitable for a gasoline station and the total cost for the physical building was around $2,000 dollars.

We opened for business sometime in December of 1945. The large sign painted on the front of the service station read: "***Jack R. Griffin Service Station—Veteran***". I had signed a three-year contract with the Sinclair Oil Company and in exchange, they furnished the gasoline tanks, pumps, an air compressor, a hydraulic lift and cement slab, neon sign, and enough paint to coat the entire building. After three years, Standard Oil of Kentucky offered me a more attractive business deal and I changed to Standard Oil. The post-war economy was booming and our business was better than we had hoped for. Our second child, Jimmy was born in the early fall of 1947. When Detroit produced the 1947, line of automobiles, we purchased a brand new 1947, model Fleetline Chevrolet, 2-door sedan. Then we built a new home behind the service station and business kept getting better. We bought brand new furniture but Adele didn't like the new automatic washing machine since she claimed that it used too much soap and water.

We had sufficient land area for the station, our home and for a small trailer park area with hook-ups. The post war era was one of increased prosperity and mobility and new technologies made it possible for many Americans to travel in ways not previously known. New automobiles and travel trailers became more visible on the highways and my gas station catered to these travelers. In addition to full service, i.e. gasoline fill-ups, checking oil and other engine fluid levels, cleaning windshields, and checking tire pressures; I also greased cars, changed oil, filters and fan belts, fixed flats, and did light mechanic work. We offered a variety of consumer products for sale such as groceries, soda pops, some auto parts, oil and other automobile lubricants, cold beer, tobacco products, some groceries, ice cream, and candies. We sold everything we could make a monetary profit off of.

I kept our place of business spotless inside and outside and our sign "*Clean Restrooms*" was no stretch of the imagination. I believed in full service to the customer and maintaining the Men's and Ladies restrooms clean and stocked was a priority. Due to the conditions of segregation across the nation in the 1940's, some service stations in the states only had two restrooms and many stations had three. Specifically, they were designated for Men, Ladies and Colored. Many Black people usually avoided service stations with only two restrooms in our area of Florida. If Black people stopped at my gasoline station and needed to go to the restroom they would have to go to the woods across the road. I was prejudiced due to not being a born-again Christian. I didn't have a free drinking-water fountain at our gas station for anyone since we sold cold sodas and beer. Regardless of who arrived thirsty, I was operating a business to make money and drinks weren't free. We had a juke box machine and sometimes after 9:00 on Saturday nights, we would invite some of our so-called friends and associates over, turn off the outside lights and with just a small light on the inside, trip the music machine, drink beer and whiskey and dance the night away. We thought we were just really having fun.

We had a lot of church going people that traded with us and many of them would stop by the station on Sunday mornings to get gasoline or to leave a tire to be fixed, and go on their way to church. I remember a Baptist deacon by the name of Arrington who would stop by on occasion and drink down two cold beers the fastest that any one could and then go on his way. A good friend, Mr. Smith who was against alcoholic beverages, rebuked me one day about selling beer. He put his hand on the icebox and said: *"Jack, why don't you quit selling this stuff"*? His honesty and serious demeanor made me shake in my shoes and his statement made me really think about what I was doing. I knew in my heart that selling beer and trafficking in strong drink was wrong but the profits were so good. After thinking it over, I later told Mr. Smith that I would quit selling beer when my beverage license expired and I kept my word.

God was beginning to deal with me in a personal way. As I said before, I had tried to pray to God while I was overseas in France. I had tried to pray in a round about fashion but they were petitions of convenience to allow me to get out of the war and to get home safely. Many soldiers have prayed this type of prayer while in the service of their country and while perhaps there is no lack of sincerity, such prayer requests are usually of a brief and transitory nature. After

I arrived back at home safe and pretty much intact except for my teeth, I forgot about some of those emotional promises I had made to God about living right if He allowed me to get home. It seems that I was worse off spiritually after the war than before.

On April 1, 1948, my precious mother, Bashie Keel Griffin passed away and it had an effect on me such as no other experience. I was holding her hand as the final breath left her body and she began to grow cold. When I took a last look at her face in the casket, I realized that she was gone and never coming back. I wept bitterly and realized full well that I was not yet ready to die. I want to remind the reader that of all the church going people that traded with us including church workers and officers and family members, no one had ever personally talked to me about the condition of my soul. It appears that no one had ever taken the time to ask me about whether I was saved or not nor had anyone discussed with me the eternal destiny of my soul. No one in my family or among my friends had ever tried to get me to come to Jesus Christ. All I had ever heard from friends and relatives was: "Join the church and be faithful to the denomination"! My heart was getting harder in terms of spiritual things and heavy smoking along with the drinking was beginning to take its toll. I was filled with the wrong spirits and tobacco smoke but that may not have concerned anyone at the time.

When the year 1949, came around, I had turned thirty-five years of age and Adele and I were making plans for the future. We would lay awake at night and make plans for the next day or for the days ahead. I usually got up before daylight and I would jump out of bed with my wheels spinning. We worked long, hard hours, seven days a week and managed our resources very well. I recall one occasion after we had been in business about three years, I heard a plane buzzing low overhead and I saw the pilot dipping his plane's wings. I figured he wanted to land on the highway in front of our station so I sent some person up the road and another person down the road in order to stop traffic. The pilot landed his plane and taxied up to the Premium pump and put in about fifteen gallons. I put in a quart of oil and he took off on the highway. Talk about customers dropping in for full service, we were there for business. By late 1949, I was well on my way to becoming a successful and respected businessman in the Chiefland community and area. We were completely out of debt and materially speaking, things were going very well for Adele and I. We had two sons and a good business but no spiritual life at all.

I recall that a group of traveling Christians stopped at my gas station about that time with their cars and travel trailers. I was impressed by their honest modesty and sincere Biblical convictions and inquired as to where they came from and where they were going. This was my first contact with the Baptist Purity people from a neighboring community called Salem, Florida.

God is longsuffering, merciful and is not willing that any should perchance perish in a devil's hell. God had plans for our lives and He was about to do something that would completely change my life for time and eternity. In His infinite love and mercy, God sent a man all the way from Kentucky who would obey the dutiful call of Gospel Evangelism to tell me about the Lord Jesus Christ and finally address the matter of my soul's eternal destiny. It seems strange and out of place in Christian America that no one had ever taken the time to do this for me. Is this possible in America with so many faiths, churches, preachers, and religious denominations all around us?

The Ivy Oma & Bashie Griffin Family at Chiefland, 1937-1939

Jack & Miss Willa Fae Nettles "hobo" a train near Chiefland, 1933

Jack using a surveyor's transit with the Civilian Conservation
Corps crew in Holmes County, Florida, 1933-1935

Bashie and Ivy Oma "Poppa" Griffin at the
Riteway Service Station at Chiefland, Florida, 1937-1939

The Griffin family posing in front of the
Riteway Service Station, at Chiefland, Florida, 1937-1939

Mrs. Anna Adele Griffin holding Johnny
with our 1939, Chevrolet at the Riteway Station in Chiefland

Jack, Adele and Hellis Griffin at the Riteway Station, 1937-1939

Jack, Johnny and Adele in Pop's yard near Chiefland, 1942

Byrd, Johnny, and Jack Griffin
in military uniform, in Pop's yard, December 1942

A brief reunion in front of tent #17 near Bath, England- 1944,
Left to Right- unknown, Byrd, Jack and unknown

Corporal- Jack R. Griffin in Paris, France on December 8, 1944

Jack R. Griffin- Veteran- Service Station at Chiefland, Florida
in the spring of 1948. Left to Right: Jack, Uncle Hard Harrison,
Adele with Johnny and Jim Griffin.

Oma Harrison in front of the Griffin Service Station, 1946-1947

SEVEN

My Conversion

"Without Faith, it is impossible to please God."
(Hebrews 11:6)

Gilbert, Jim and Julian Turner lived in Chiefland and they had operated the bus station and a restaurant there. Jim Turner later became Levy County Sheriff and was in office when I was arrested in 1958. Julian would joke all the time and on occasions he would bring a nanny goat into his restaurant and milk her for a laugh. The faithful evangelist from Kentucky was Brother Julian Turner who for years had been an incurable alcoholic and he had tried everything from the American Red Cross to the Veteran's Administration but to no avail. Julian had been my friend and a former companion in sin as a drinking buddy. He had been in an old fashioned Gospel meeting in 1949, got under conviction and gave his heart to Christ. The Lord soon called him into the ministry and he went to Asbury College in Wilmore, Kentucky to prepare for the work of the Gospel of Christ. He was not afraid to speak out against sin and he would preach the Gospel in a plain way.

In early March of 1950, Julian Turner came to our mutually adopted hometown of Chiefland, Florida. I can never thank the Lord enough for sending this man of God to tell me that the life I was living would not be good enough for me to make it to heaven.

Brother Julian Turner preached a series of messages in the Methodist Church in nearby Williston and Adele and I would close our gas station before sun down and drive over so as not to miss any part of the preaching. He was a plain preacher, bold in the Lord and told it like it was without fear or favor. He preached about heaven and he preached about hell and I realized that God had prepared both places. God prepared heaven for His saints and He prepared hell for the devil and his angels and the wicked that reject Christ. God has done everything possible to keep us from going to hell. God has sent His only Son named Jesus of Nazareth to die on the cross to redeem us from sin and to keep us out of hell. At this time in my life, I did not know this one, true God. I had heard a little *about* Him and His Son- Jesus Christ but now I was about to *know* Him, manifested as God the Father, God the Son and God the Holy Spirit.

After hearing Julian preach one night and deeply under conviction, I took Adele's hand and we made our way to an old fashioned altar. We both got down on our knees and I began to pray. I really didn't know how to pray and the prayer I prayed didn't go any higher than the ceiling. I found out later why. I found that I was trying to hold on to the world with one hand and trying at the same time to reach out and take hold of God. This concept of fence straddling simply doesn't work at all. I realized that we must completely let go of this sinful world including our selfish materialistic plans for the future. We must completely put our all on God's altar. We must completely put our family, our material things and all our concerns in God's hands and denying ourselves, take up our cross and follow Jesus. *"What things were gain to me, those I counted loss for Christ... I press toward the mark for the prize of the high calling of God in Christ Jesus."* (Philippians 3:7 & 14) In reality, it is all or none for Jesus Christ. We must make a complete surrender to the Lord Jesus Christ and allow Him to have His way in our lives and we are obligated to exercise our faith. This is just exactly what I finally did and this is the way it happened.

The night that Adele and I went to the altar, I didn't pray through and get saved. I was bewildered. I was deeply under the conviction of the Holy Spirit and I wanted more than anything to make heaven my home in eternity. But on the other hand, I had all these sound business plans for the future. After all, I felt that I had lost almost three years in the military and I needed to make it up by doing some double time in business. I felt that I deserved to make lots of money. After the church services, I went around for several days like I was in a trance. I was halted between two opinions and as Rev. Thomas Griffin phrased the concept: "*It was like a man looking one way but rowing another.*" (Griffin, p. 101) The devil didn't want to let me go since he had completely motivated my life for 35 years.

I didn't know what was really going on in the spiritual realm between God and Satan. I know now that spiritual things in the war for my soul were fast approaching a climax. I was fixing to pass from the realm of death into life, out of spiritual darkness into the light of the glory world, and out of the clutches of the devil into God's kingdom. This all happened on the 15th day of March 1950, at about 6:00 A. M. which was the regular time for opening the gas station. I unlocked the door and I seemed to freeze in my tracks. I sensed a unique feeling in my inner man as if someone was talking to me but not in an audible voice. A higher power was impressing upon my heart and mind the urgent message of repentance and salvation. I know now that it was the mighty Holy Spirit of God whose presence was real and powerful. He impressed upon my heart that I needed to surrender to Christ *now* and that it was *now* or never and that my time was running out. A vision began running through my mind like a full color, panoramic motion picture of my whole sinful life. It appeared as if God was showing my past life on a big screen. I was greatly impressed that God was fully aware of all the details of my life and that He was concerned about my spiritual well-being. He revealed His great concern for the little sins in my life as well as the big sins. I didn't think that it really mattered with God about my little white lies, smoking cigarettes, and having a few drinks with my buddies. I found out that God is very much concerned about our little sins the same as our big sins. If we confess our little sins to God, He will also forgive our larger, more serious sins as well. This is God's intervention for sin.

While this entire struggle was going on in my mind and soul, it seemed that God gave me a pre-view of the Lake of Fire. I could see many poor lost souls burning in the flames of hell, crying for water: "*Just a drop of water!*", but to no avail. It seems that for some moments, I continued to hear the wailing and crying of these lost souls. According to the Holy Bible, they will continue to cry for water throughout endless eternity. No one in hell will have any friends and it is a place of eternal outer darkness. Many of us already have loved ones who have landed in hell and are doomed for eternity. It is an unpleasant thought but true according to the Word of God.

I stood there in my service station doorway, and my legs became weak. I felt the need to pray and I wanted to find a place to kneel. All I wanted at that time was to be alone with God and tell Him how truly sorrowful I was for all my sins. I closed the door of the station and sank to my knees over against the inside wall and I began to cry out to God. With tears streaming down my face, I began confessing my sins directly to God. I don't know how long I prayed but I knew my prayers were reaching up to God's throne room of Grace and Mercy. The answer soon came back and in a moment's time, my sins were gone, forgiven by Faith in the cleansing power of the Blood of the Lamb of God. As my sins were lifted away, I felt as light as a feather and for a moment it seemed that I was floating in the air. I rose to my feet and while crying and laughing at the same time, I began praising and thanking God for saving my soul. I knew that I was born-again into God's family at that time and on that spot with the promise of eternal life. I was born-again in an instant and God baptized me in the Holy Spirit and fire. Every person must have this experience in order to be with God in heaven. The Lord Jesus Christ Himself declared emphatically: "*Except a man be born again, he cannot see the kingdom of God*". (St. John 3:3) Nothing else will replace the new birth. Indisputably, this imperative heavenly commandment supercedes any earthly denominational persuasion or religious creed. Man changes, society changes and the world changes in fickle and nefarious ways but God the Father, God the Son and God the Holy Spirit never change. "*Jesus Christ, the same yesterday, today and forever.*" (Hebrews 13:8)

This was the beginning of my new life and of course, I wanted to immediately tell everybody about what had happened to me and I started by running over to our house just behind the service station to tell Adele. As I tried to tell her of my new found joy, she gave me a funny look and as if to say you must have had a bad dream. My initial testimony of becoming a born-again Christian elicited no plaudits from any worldly friends or any family members regardless how close or distant. Every born-again Christian has the desire and drive to tell others about this wonderful Savior and Lord, if not, something is wrong. When a person is really saved by God's Grace, there will be a compelling drive to share Christ with others. If a person doesn't have this desire to share the Gospel even some time after conversion, something is wrong. They need to be genuinely born-again or return to their first love. Jesus Christ offered His beaten, ravaged body on the old rugged cross of Calvary as a dying sacrifice for the sins of the entire world. Upon our acceptance of Jesus as our personal Savior, we may offer our bodies as a living sacrifice in His service. God wants us to give Him our bodies so that He as Emmanuel may dwell in our lives and in our conscience and be glorified. This is as the Apostle phrased it, having the mind of Christ with a conscience as free and clear as God's. Even children can comprehend God's simple plan of salvation.

Now that I was a child of God, the Holy Spirit began to work in my new life. He began to show me the things that please our Heavenly Father. I had smoked cigarettes for about twenty years and now, the Holy Spirit clearly showed me in the same hour that I wouldn't need to smoke tobacco or sell it anymore. He impressed upon my heart that God's children weren't destined to be smokers but that we are to be on fire for Him. During my old life, I had drank beer and liquors but now in my new life no other "spirits" were needed, the Holy Spirit was my Comforter, Guide and Teacher. The joy unspeakable of the Lord Jesus is a Biblical reality and is not manifested in human hedonism and bacchanalian practices. Scriptures such as: *"Woe to him that giveth his neighbor drink, that puttest thy bottle to him and maketh him drunken also, that thou mayest look on their nakedness"*, found in Habakkuk 2:15, became the Biblical basis of specific Christian convictions, an essential part of my new lifestyle.

The temporal material things of this world began to grow strangely dim and unessential. From the very day of my conversion to Christ, I lost all interest in modern sports and other worldly attractions. Things like the Hollywood movie shows, partying and dancing, working on Sunday and going to the public bathing beaches became obsolete in importance. These things are of the world and contrary to God's will. I still adhere to the conviction that modern commercial sports programs are incompatible with Biblical Christianity. It is no secret that the highly visible sports world involves drug abuse, gross immorality, extreme materialism, profanity, violence, and an excessively competitive spirit. These elements dominate the flesh and destroy any possible connection to any worthwhile spiritual life. In his Panegyricus, Isocrates declared: *"If the athletes were to acquire twice the strength they possess, no advantage would accrue to other men; but if one man were to conceive a wise thought all would reap the enjoyment of his understanding who were willing to share in it"*. (Freese, p. 2) He was completely right and the same valid argument can be made even today. The Word of God plainly declares in First Thessalonians, chapter 5, verses 21 and 22; that Christ's disciples are to: *"abstain from all appearance of evil"*. Wise men still follow Jesus Christ.

It is not that my religion won't let me do this or that; I simply have no desire to commit any act contrary to God's plan and will. The holiness of heart and purity in the Christian's lifestyle are directives from God, not multiple choice options in free moral agency. The deep things of God are a Biblical reality, not legalism or Phariseeism. I soon found that I began to love my enemies and that I wanted to do what was right and good for everyone for Jesus sake. I was no longer motivated to be prejudiced in any way against anyone. From the beginning of my new life until the present day, I have had no animus toward anyone. God's agape love is universal.

Before my conversion, I had been very selfish. Now that I was a new Christian, the Holy Spirit reminded me of how I had been mean-spirited toward a Black man who lived across the railroad tracks in Hardee Town. This Black man made a living by doing odd jobs around the community such as plowing people's gardens, cutting and hauling firewood for people to use in their fireplaces and so on. This man had two horses to pull his wagon and to plow with and having no pastureland of his own for them to graze in, he would turn them out to graze at night. They finally made their way up to our gas station to graze on our lawn. They would leave their hoof prints in the soft, sandy Florida soil and this made me very unhappy. I quickly told this man to do something with his horses because if they came up to my place again, I would shoot them dead. I would have done what I said and the Black man must have understood my intent from my demeanor since his horses never bothered us again.

At this time, having been born-again, I had the precious love of Jesus in my heart. God had forgiven me of a sinful past and now I had the Spirit of God and I was obliged to love and forgive others. One day soon after, I saw this man coming down the road in his wagon. The Holy Spirit began reminding me of how I had done him wrong and that I must apologize for my action. The devil was already telling me that he was *only* a Black man but as a child of God, I must please the Father so I said: "*Lord, I will do it*". I walked out to approach him as he drove up in his old farm wagon. By the look on his face, he was afraid that I was about to do him harm. He stopped his horses and as I looked up, tears were streaming down my face. It was obvious that he didn't know what was going on. I asked him if he would forgive me for the harsh words I had said and his face lit up and with a big smile he said: "*Yas Suh! Yas suh, I forgives yuh*". From then on, he was one of the best friends I had in Chiefland, Florida.

During the month of April 1950, I was baptized by immersion in the baptistry of the Beaver Street Baptist church in Jacksonville, Florida. Afterwards, I had such a heavy burden to tell others about this new found friend- Jesus Christ my Lord that I would go out on the streets of Chiefland and preach the unsearchable riches of Christ over my public address system and large metal trumpet speakers. Then I would go to other towns and in time, to other states, and to other countries to preach the Word of God. I was compelled by the Holy Spirit to warn the wicked, to encourage the repentant, and to build up the faith of the righteous. To preach the Gospel is to first live what is preached and oftentimes God qualifies those He calls and ignores those who think they alone are qualified to be called.

This was exactly the case with Thomas Griffin who felt that his lack of formal education and training was an impediment to ministry. God called him; he humbly obeyed and impacted many lives across a wide swath of the nation. *"I began to have a strong desire that all men could know and feel what I thought and know. I felt peace of mind with God and a great desire to see man cultivate those principles that would promote their good and shun those that would injure them such as swearing, lying, drinking and living in a state of irreligion. I looked back at the dreadful dilemma I had been in myself and felt the wages of sin was death and that sin was no longer a visionary thing and that so many of mankind were not making any pretension to try and do right but moving in the opposite direction. The whole world with some exceptions, were lying in the wicked one and going in direct opposition to the commands of God and I thought much about the dreadful condition of men. I was impressed I ought to tell them what condition they were in and show them how they might experience this change and the happy consequences...love, peace of mind, peace with God, peace toward all men, peace in life, in death, and to all eternity. If they continued as they were in a state of uncertainty, slaves to folly, pursuing a cause piercing them with sorrow, it was only the prelude of a more dreadful fate that awaits them hereafter."* (Griffin, p. 58 & 59)

Sometime between March and August of 1950, my first cousin Bell Harrison wrote an article in the local newspaper, The Levy County Journal commenting about how I preached on the streets. He mentioned something about a fellow preaching like a donkey and compared him to Balaam's Ass braying. He was fairly accurate in his assumption since I don't preach what men say but I preach what God says. Well, even Balaam's donkey had a message from God but according to the Biblical story; carnal man was blind to the spirit realm and could not receive the Divine message until his eyes were opened. I never have made any claim to having the status of being God's Prophet but I did endeavor to fulfill the work of an Evangelist in my home, my community, in my state and in my nation as well as to people in other countries. I rejoiced that if God could use a donkey's mouth to speak the truth, surely He could use my lips to preach the Gospel of Jesus Christ.

I started closing the gasoline station on Sundays and began attending church services. Adele would go with me if I went to the Baptist Church. She told me in her own words: *"I am a Baptist and*

I will be a Baptist until I die", proving there is some truth in the adage of one being a "dyed in the wool" religious devotee. When we arrived at the church, she would take a last draw on her cigarette and throw the butt on the ground and exhale as we went up to the door. When I was saved, I wanted to be in church especially on the Lord's Day. At first, I took a real interest in the Baptist Church in Chiefland and I would even close the gasoline station in order to go and help work on building a new Sunday school room. We attended this Baptist church for about four months and I even helped my Dad and my brother Hellis in carpenter work and painting. I began to see that there was not much spiritual life in the denomination for me. On Wednesday night prayer meetings, there would be the regular eight or nine in routine attendance. Most prayers on average seemed weaker on the spiritual scale than those of groaning, weeping peni-tents thrown across a Methodist mourner's bench in a sincere search of God's grace and mercy. When on the festive occasion of a meal such as a big fish fry, watermelon festival or some form of entertain-ment, there would be a full house. I couldn't help but notice that the main church sanctuary would be dark and empty but the recreation hall would be all lit up and full of people. The Lord impressed on my heart that this denomination was not solely representative of His Church, the Ecclesia of the New Testament so I permanently left the largest Baptist denomination and began to seek out a more spiritual place to worship. This was about the time that we had almost gone out of business in the gasoline station and had put it up for sale.

It is quite possible that there were and are some real Christians among the various Baptist groups as well as among other organized church fellowships but it is indisputable that all existing religious denominations are merely man-made entities. Our Lord Jesus Christ came to this sinful world, was born in a manger, was crucified and died on an old rugged cross at Calvary. Jesus shed His blood to save us from our sins, not in our sins. Jesus was raised from the dead, not to build any political empires or religious denominations and yet He is head of His Church. I was considered as something of a fanatic from the beginning of my conversion because of my spiritual convictions. Some of the community perceptions and judgments were based on the examples of my changed behavior such as when

I was saved, I abruptly stopped smoking cigarettes and three days later, I stopped selling tobacco products altogether. Instead of getting drunk, I preached strongly against using alcoholic beverages.

I suppose I was looked upon as some sort of killjoy for my clean break with worldly involvements but the bottom line was simply that my new life was to be a Christian role model to my wife and sons, to my extended family and the community. I stopped allowing our boys to go to the worldly movies and I told them the truth about Halloween, the Easter bunny and fictional characters such as Santa Claus and many comic book and cartoon personalities. Such fantasies are lies and as a born-again Christian, I could no more lie to my own children than fly to Mars. I felt very strongly as a parent that I needed to ensure that my children did not become cornucopia children. I knew that my cogent responsibility as a father and provider included emphasizing spiritual matters and maintaining a material balance in the home. I desired to raise the children God blessed us with, to be in good health, to have reasonable expectations, to learn the work ethic, to be ready for the real world, to have a real knowledge of the Bible and to know Jesus Christ. Consequently, we had regular prayer and Bible reading in our home. In addition to reading Bible stories, I read many books to my children including Pilgrim's Progress, Hurlbut's Story of the Bible for Young and Old, Through Gates of Splendor, and the stories of Samuel Morris and Sgt. DeShazer. We studied the Thompson Chain Reference Bible from start to finish. I believe the quality time that I spent with my children studying Christianity was the best possible investment of my time and efforts and I do not regret it nor do I apologize for it.

I strongly believed in the necessity to make voluntary restitution and to ask forgiveness of those people that I had wronged in the past. Eighteen years after my hobo trip by train to Chicago, I had a new life to live and one day I was talking to a friend about my past trip. The Holy Spirit impressed upon my mind that I had not paid for the train transportation so I searched for the mailing addresses of each ticket agent of each of the four railroad systems I had ridden on. I mailed each one a letter of explanation and stated that I wanted to pay for my trip taken at their expense and I received a reply from each company agent. Three agents sent me bills totaling forty-dollars and the fourth agent's written response was that he was glad that I had gotten saved and that I didn't owe anything. Voluntary restitution is a witness of Christ's love and forgiveness. Furthermore, I would take most any kind of work available to supplement our income and maintain the flexibility of Evangelistic work. Soon after my conversion I worked in the fields for .75 cents an hour and I even started having church services in the gasoline station but it just didn't work out.

I wanted to tell everybody about the Lord Jesus Christ and what He had done for me. I started by telling my customers about the risen Christ. I also wanted to know more about God's Word and one of the first steps I made very shortly after my conversion was to buy a precious copy of the King James 1611, translation of the Holy Bible. I had never owned a Bible and I was completely ignorant of its contents so in my sincere interest and zeal, I began an earnest, regular and systematic study of the Scriptures for several hours each day. I visualized the children of Israel traveling across the Sinai with their numerous families and large herds of cattle. The Scriptures were so real to my heart and mind that I could almost hear the cattle lowing, the bleating of the sheep and the wagon wheels creaking as they plodded along a desert track. I pictured the dust rising from the animal's hooves, the cloud by day and the pillar of fire by night.

I became so fascinated in reading the Word of God that I would not hear a car drive up to the gas pumps. After a few minutes some of the customers would drive away. Other customers would ask for a pack of their favorite brand of cigarettes, or snuff, pipe or chewing tobacco and when I tried to explain the reason that I no longer sold tobacco products, some customers would walk out of the station mumbling in a low tone: "*He's losing his mind over religion*". I was definitely losing interest in operating a gasoline station since it was demanding too much of my time and just making a lot of money was no longer the primary focus of my new life. I began to feel a tugging in my heart to become a Missionary. I wanted to tell every one I could about Jesus, and about how he came from heaven to save us from our sins so that we could live with Him in the Father's house. Now, instead of expanding our business, I wanted to sell what we already had. Adele didn't agree and it took a whole year for her to change her mind. God works in mysterious ways and not always overnight.

I rented the service station out and in September 1950, I enrolled at the Asbury College in Wilmore, Kentucky. I wanted to study the Bible with other Christians and also to be with Brother Julian Turner who had led me to Jesus. I wanted to be part of a group of Christians in Bible study and in the daily application of our Faith. Upon enrolling, we were given a new copy of the 1934, edition of the Thompson Chain Reference Bible and a copy of Dispensational Truth by Clarence Larkin. We experienced a wonderful outpouring of God's Holy Spirit at Asbury College the first week of school. There were no classes all that week and prayer meetings were going day and night. It was a little of heaven on earth. We spent substantial time in a serious study of the Bible and church history. I came away with a great appreciation of the Early Church, Reformation, and Revival periods. I wholeheartedly agree with Rev. Thomas Griffin's assessment of the Wesley's ministry and his feeling concerning himself runs parallel with mine. *"Through the mercy and goodness of God, I have passed the toils, cares, and anxieties of 1843. I have been on the brink of the grave to all human appearance and at the close of the year I have read the life of Mr. Charles Wesley. Oh what a man of God he was and it was a blessing to me. Such as; I shall thank God in time and eternity. I believe I have clearer views of the plan of Salvation than I ever had. I have peace with God and shall wait the dispensations of Providence to wind up the few years I shall have on earth. I can truly say I have reached a period in my life, I am not only willing to be little and unknown but I covet it. I can truly say- Thy will be done."* (Griffin, p. 186) I was at Asbury College for only six weeks since my wife wrote requesting that I come back to Florida. She was afraid that she was going to have a nervous breakdown. I went home immediately and helped her through this time of crisis. Adele hadn't gotten saved when I did and she didn't have any interest in the Lord's work. She still smoked cigarettes and didn't want to go with me to church or out to evangelize.

God did not give up on us and our third child was Paul, born in early 1951. I still wanted to study the Bible in a formal setting with other believers so in about 1951, I enrolled closer to home in a Pentecostal school, Faith Temple in St. Petersburg, Florida; founded and directed by Pastor Charles M. Leaming. On one occasion, another Bible student at Faith Temple asked me to accompany him to visit a Jewish Synagogue in Saint Petersburg, Florida. We attended a Saturday service and we were invited to partake in a fellowship meal following. We both sat at the same table with several Jewish people and we began telling everybody at the table about Jesus Christ. The Rabbi heard us talking, came over to the table and with a heavy accent, addressed us in a straightforward manner: "*I will preach to my people*". I politely asked him if I could talk with him sometime. He said: "*Sometime, I will give you an hour of my precious time*", and walked away. We parted amicably. I never did get the opportunity to talk with the Rabbi.

While I was at Faith Temple School, Evangelist Oral Roberts came to Tampa, Florida to conduct a crusade with his large Gospel tent. He soon discovered our Bible school and he contacted Brother Leaming about having us students serve as helpers in the prayer tent. I remember the afternoon before the first night's meeting when one of the assistant pastors gave us a briefing in the prayer tent. He told the men to take a bath before they came to help that night and to have a fresh shave. I thought this was some very good advice. Then he turned to the ladies and simply said: "*You ladies wash your faces and leave them washed*". That meant no make up and I wonder if any one connected to the same ministry even considers this today.

Our duties were to talk with people seeking spiritual help who had come to pray. We would kneel beside folks and help them to talk with God in prayer from their hearts. We sought to help honest people to pray the sincere type of prayer that God would hear and answer. I had been a Christian about two years and I believed that Evangelist Oral Roberts was a real man of God and that he had the gift of healing. If anyone wanted to receive healing, they would have to be at the meeting the night before to get a coupon. I got my coupon and was in the prayer line the next night. Brother Oral Roberts would sit in a chair and a long line of people who wanted to be healed would pass in front of his chair. I had suffered most all of my life with acid reflux and had been discharged from the military with a forty-percent disability. When I finally arrived at where Brother Oral Roberts was sitting, he laid his big hand on my forehead and I knew something had happened. Thank God, for four years I had no symptoms and could eat most anything I wanted. About two years later in about 1954, I attended another Oral Roberts tent meeting in Jacksonville, Florida. I still believe what he sincerely preached at that time. I finished a semester of studies at Faith Temple and then went back home to be with Adele.

It was about a year later that she did reluctantly agree to make a trip out west in our newly acquired travel trailer. I was impressed by the need to minister to the American Indians in Arizona and New Mexico and anywhere else we could find indigenous tribes. Adele, John, Jim, Paul and I traveled through Oklahoma, New Mexico and Arizona to Phoenix. In 1951, or 1952, I worked in a citrus packing plant for about three months and Adele and I picked Arizona cotton a time or two. From Mesa, Arizona, we went to minister among the Papago tribe near Ajo, Arizona. After about three months, Adele was tired of traveling and demanded that I take her back to Florida or she would take the bus back home. I drove back through Tucson and the south west as fast as I could in our 1947, Chevrolet pulling the trailer. Our first mission trip wasn't as successful as I had hoped for but it was the beginning. When we arrived at my Dad's house near Chiefland, Adele took the three boys and went to her mother's place at Branford in nearby Suwannee County. We finally sold the gasoline station for $7,000 to Mr. Singleton Barker who had operated a store and had been the Postmaster at Hardee Town. I had given my wife $4,000.00 dollars upon selling the service station in Chiefland. She soon hired a lawyer who brought up a case in the Circuit Court of Suwannee County, Florida for separate child custody of our children. I was soon informed that I had lost all my legal rights to my children and that I had no visitation rights. It was very clear that a conflict of spiritual interests had arisen in our family. It wasn't the first time in history that a theological conflict contributed to a divided Griffin household.

EIGHT

Deep Methodist Roots

"The world is my parish." – John Wesley

More than one of our Methodist ancestors had a serious disagreement with family members of another theological persuasion. A relevant quote from Bishop Galloway based upon the Thomas Griffin Journal reveals some of the theological conflict within our Griffin family in Georgia. The quote is cited from the book: A Way Through the Wilderness by William C. Davis.

> In one family the father called himself "a highland or dry-footed Baptist"; the mother professed Methodism but went to the Baptist church to keep her husband happy. Their son Thomas Griffin, in 1808, heard one of the itinerants preach, went home a convert, bent on heeding the call to preach himself, and he started with his father, no easy task.
> (Davis, p. 138, Harper Collins Pubs.)

The conflict between John Griffin and his son Thomas became so acute that John would not speak to his son. It wasn't long before Thomas left home in 1810, on an emotional note to begin preaching in the South Carolina Methodist Conference.

Very little accurate genealogical knowledge of our family history had been passed along to us in Florida. With my contributions and assistance, the extensive genealogical work done by my youngest son Silas has provided a detailed overview of our Griffin family tree and branches. We have discovered that a significant number of our Andrews, Barnett, Ford, Hubbert, Malone and Smith relatives including many of our Griffin ancestors in the states of Virginia, Georgia, Alabama, Mississippi and Louisiana, were of the Wesleyan Methodist persuasion. My third great paternal grandfather, John Griffin, a retired Revolutionary War veteran from Powhatan County, Virginia came with his family to Big Creek in Greene County, Georgia on January 27, 1792. He was the ancestor known to be a "highland or dry-footed Baptist"; meaning that he didn't practice the traditional Baptist mode of water baptism via immersion. This isn't the first time in our history that one or more family members held to strong personal views on religion or were apparently halted between two theological opinions. John's wife, my third great grandmother, Mrs. Mary Ann Andrews Griffin, was of the Wesleyan Methodist theological persuasion and two of their sons became Methodist preachers. Thomas Griffin, born September 24, 1787, in Cumberland County, Virginia, was converted to Christianity in a Methodist meeting in Georgia in 1808. The no longer doubting Thomas of the Griffin family testified:

"There was to be a two days' meeting held at Pope's Chapel in Oglethorpe. Hope Hull and James Russell were to hold it in connection to Benjamin Blanton. Several of our relatives, to wit- Anthony Smith and others were expected up to the meeting. My mother and myself went to meet them and of course to welcome them home. I went to laugh and to help circulate little tales that would have a bearing on the Methodists. I well recollect that I thought James Russell an enthusiast. Hope Hull came down and sang a Hymn that made the flesh tremble on me, and caused an awful sense of the hereafter to press on my mind that has not lost its charm though it was thirty-two years ago it was sung".

Let thy kingdom, blessed savior-
Come and bid our warring cease-
Come oh come, and reign forever-
God of love and prince of peace-
Visit now poor bleeding Zion-
Hear thy people moan and weep-
Day and night thy lambs are crying-
The good shepherd, feed thy sheep.

"I think it was the first time I had ever heard it sung. Mrs. Patrick broke forth and shouted. It fell on me like a shock. There was a small class there composed of the Popes, Hills, Benjamin Blanton, Mr. Turman, and William Patrick. They were a steady, orderly people and I thought well of Blanton. At night there was a meeting. My cousin Anthony Smith and the young Andrews wished to go so I went too. Russell preached and in his tremendous conclusion, he called them (the congregation) *up to be prayed for and several went. The devil rendered me indignant and after a little, left the house. My wicked lion had got disturbed in his cage. At Sunday, Hope Hull preached. He spoke like a man of God; there was a deep, marked attention among the large audience. He painted the agonies of the cross with all those tones and gestures that he was capable of. In fact, looking back after 32 years with what I have learned since, I now would pronounce it: "The Divine eloquence of the Holy Ghost" sent down from heaven. I know how I was unprepared and troubled. The meeting wound up and the next two weeks, my mind was like a pair of scales. The shortness of time- the length of eternity, a heaven lost- hell secure. The pittance of time assigned to a man on his passage from the cradle to the grave made me come to the conclusion, I would seek God.*

I returned home, found a deep washed place (gully) *into which I crept and for the first time in my life, tried to pray to God sincerely. The Wednesday following, up stairs in my father's house about 12:00, I was pressed beyond measure. I made an unconditional surrender and the language of my soul was- Save Lord! Or I perish! In this situation there appeared a powerful appeal to my soul- Believe in the Lord Jesus Christ. I believed it. I clearly saw the plan of man's*

redemption by Jesus Christ. I understood the saying of St. Peter-"If any man be in Christ, he is a new creation, old things are passed away and behold, all things have become new."
I got Benjamin Blanton to baptize me at Pope's Chapel in the winter of 1810." (Griffin- Journal, pps. 41- 46, 48, 50, 53)

William Griffin, an older brother of Thomas Griffin, was a Methodist deacon and local preacher during the early 1800's in the region of Henry County, Georgia. Two more of their brothers were also Methodists. The Griffin twins, David Andrews Griffin and Jesse Andrews Griffin, had migrated from Georgia into the Mississippi Territory before 1810, and were killed in an ambush in November of 1813, by the Creek Red Stick Warriors at the Bashi Skirmish in Clarke County, Alabama. A significant Methodist revival was experienced among the early settlers of Clarke County, Alabama in 1812, and 1813, and this spiritual awakening on the American frontier was due in part to the efforts of the four stalwart Methodist missionaries handpicked in 1810, by Bishop Francis Asbury and sent out as Ambassadors of Jesus Christ. Reverend Thomas Griffin had spent two years preaching in the Brunswick circuit in the South Carolina Conference before moving into his itinerant preaching appointment in the Ouachita circuit in the Louisiana Territory. He was at one time the presiding elder of the Alabama District, Mississippi Conference, Tombecbee being one of the charges in this district. In his book: "A History of Methodism" published in 1893, author Bishop Holland McTyeire provides an overview of the ministry of Rev. Thomas Griffin and his fellow Wesleyan Methodist missionaries.

In the spring of 1812, four young men on horseback, take the road to the West. They are missionaries from South Carolina— Thomas Griffin, Richmond Nolley, Lewis Hobbs, and Drury Powell. At Milledgeville, Georgia, they get passports to go through the Indian Nation, 350 miles; for the Creeks or Muskogees are directly in their path and to maintain peace with them, the Government is careful to keep out mischief-making men. Passing through the wilderness, crossing five rivers and lying out eleven nights, they arrive safely at the

Tombigbee Mission where Nolley's appointment was. Lewis Hobbs spent a year in the limits of the circuit Tobias Gibson had cultivated. He was a weeping prophet, a lovely spirit, and his brief ministry made a deep impression. Part of a year he labored in New Orleans where his last strength was spent. He sunk into consumption and barely got back to Georgia to die. Drury Powell preached one year beyond the river, and concluded the time had not come for those people, and returned whence he came. Thomas Griffin was assigned to the most distant and difficult post of all—the Ouachita Circuit. He proved a chosen vessel of the Lord. Few have been so honored in planting Methodism in the South-west. He lived to a good old age, and his memory is blessed by thousands. While Nolley persuaded sinners and Hobbs wept over them, Griffin made them quail and shrink, and hide their faces in fear and shame. There was a clear, metallic ring in his nature. Without the advantage of fortune or education, he made his way by stronger forces. By the camp-fire, on the forest-path, he studied. One of the saddle-bags men— to whom Western civilization is more indebted than to any other class of agents—he mastered the hardy elements of frontier life. Sagacious in judgment, decisive in action, strong in speech, generous hearted. Memorable awakenings and reformations of notorious and hopeless sinners occurred under his ministry. He would "get on the sinner's track" as he phrased it, and press him close, calling conscience to witness as he went along. His language was often more forcible than elegant. The presumptuous sinner was "one of your gospel-slighting, heaven-neglecting, God-provoking, devil-daring, hell-deserving rebels against the majesty of the universe." The drunkard, in his estimation, "was a far worse character than the frantic suicide who would take a pistol and blow out his brains, thus ridding his family of a pest, and leaving his property for their maintenance; whereas the drunkard, after disgracing his family with his besotted example, afflicting them with his drunken revels, wasting his property, breaking the heart of his wife, and hanging his poor, ragged, uneducated children on the horns of poverty, is in the end a self-murderer." If he had occasion to hold up the superannuated debauchee in order to show the way of the transgressor is hard, he would describe him as "the very frazzle ends of humanity; his debauched carcass would disgrace a wolf-trap if put in it for bait." His scathing denunciation of vice stirred the ire and resentment of the wicked. They had driven off Powell, and a leader of roughs resolved, upon the reports that had reached him, to drive off Griffin. This man went to one of his appointments, listened to a terribly searching and courageous discourse, and after the service was over remarked to some one who had heard his threat that "Mr. Griffin improved on further acquaintance, and he reckoned it was best to have a few such preachers in the country, so he would not interrupt him." Thomas Griffin found a good wife among the daughters of John Ford, and after presiding over districts in Louisiana, Mississippi, and Alabama, that are now Annual Conferences, he met the last enemy, as he had met all others—like a Christian hero. (McTyeire, pps. 543—546)

At one point during his early ministry in the Louisiana Territory, Thomas Griffin stated, *"The difficulties we had to encounter were almost incredible"*, and he literally wore out his only pair of pants traveling in the wilderness and preaching throughout Louisiana. Being a close friend of Thomas Griffin, Rev. Richmond Nolley also traveled in the Louisiana Territory and froze to death on the evangelistic trail on November 25, 1814, at 24 years of age. He is buried at the Nolley Memorial Methodist Church in Jena, Louisiana and his grave monument there reads: *"Rev. Richmond Nolley (1784—1814) Pioneer Methodist Preacher, First Methodist Circuit Rider who died in Louisiana, died of freezing and exposure near Jena while trying to reach his next charge. "Be ye doers of the Word and not hearers only."* How many professing Christians in the 21st Century would put their very lives on the line for Jesus? These four stalwarts answered God's call to preach and served God with all their hearts and minds to the end of their time on earth.

Methodist Episcopal Bishop Charles B. Galloway wrote an essay entitled: "Thomas Griffin; A Boanerges of the Early Southwest." This biographical sketch of the life and ministry of Rev. Thomas Griffin was published in Publications of the Mississippi Historical Society, Volume VII, in 1903. Bishop Galloway states: *"Stories of his quaint sayings, striking proverbs, vivid illustrations, and terrific excoriations of popular vices have been handed down from father to son in all the regions of his public ministry. Mr. Griffin reared an interesting family and gave to his children the best collegiate advantages. The last entry in his manuscript journal was January 1, 1850. "I now see the first of 1850, but much doubt my seeing its close. If I fall this year may I have grace sufficient to my day and especially the dying day; and may the providence of God be over my children, is my sincere prayer"*. (Galloway, p. 170)

God sent a spiritual revival in the Tombigbee region that preceded and endured throughout the Creek Indian War of 1813, in Southwest Alabama. Our merciful God foreknew the terrible outcome of this conflict and sent His Word by His faithful servants to save many souls of people that would be killed in the Creek War. One hundred years before I was born in the same area of Clarke County, Alabama, God had sent one of my Methodist ancestors and three of his itinerant Christian companions to preach the Gospel all throughout the wilderness region of the Tombigbee River of Alabama and Mississippi. Their spiritual influence endures to the present time for Indian, African, Anglo, French and Spanish ethnicities alike. One of David Andrew Griffin's sons was William Griffin, born in 1812, at Wood's Bluff in Clarke County along the Tombigbee, River.

Some primary source historical records list the names of young men from the Andrews, Bird, Ford, Griffin, Holland, Johnson, Malone, Mims and Sample families from Virginia, Georgia, Alabama and Mississippi as being involved in the War for Texas Independence in the mid-1830's. Being an orphan, single and 24 years old, our William Griffin may have come to Texas in 1835, possibly accompanied by some collateral relatives and he could have participated in the battle of San Jacinto as a soldier in Colonel Edward Burleson's 1st Regiment Infantry, Company A, under Major General Sam Houston. With a Private William Griffin, a single, 24-year old farmer from

Alabama listed in Company A, was 2nd Sergeant James A. Sylvester, the sole flag bearer of the Texian army at the battle of San Jacinto. Sgt. James Sylvester was personally responsible for the capture of General Santa Anna, the commander of the Mexican Army and the self-proclaimed Napoleon of the West.

Another possible relative was an early Texas pioneer named Peter Griffin, a Spanish speaking soldier in Captain Samuel O. Pettus's Company known as the San Antonio Grays in the Lafayette Battalion under Colonel James Fannin's Command at Goliad. Peter Griffin survived the Goliad massacre on March 27, 1836, by being detained as a hospital worker. These early visitors to the Texas colony were followed by a later immigration of close relations from the Dunning and Sample families to Gonzales County following the War for Texas Independence. A number of Alabamans from Clarke County and men from Mississippi were closely involved with the settlement and independence of The Republic of Texas. Later, our William Griffin was a faithful member of the Bethel Methodist Church near Choctaw Corner in Northern Clarke County, Alabama.

My conversion and pursuant growth in the Grace and knowledge of Jesus Christ was very much influenced by the same Wesleyan Methodist theology and practice of faith. This lifestyle consisted of a great deal more of commitment to Christ than mere baptism, a shallow profession of faith and church membership. Some of my other ancestors may have held a grudge against the Indians for what happened to the Griffin twins in 1813, but as a Christian, I have never felt any hatred toward the Native American Indians or toward anyone else for that matter. I am still an old-fashioned, Bible-reading, sin-socking, harmonica-playing, shouting, Wesleyan Methodist at heart, in mind and in lifestyle. The Grace of God manifested in our Lord Jesus Christ is absolutely worth preaching, praying, singing and shouting about!

NINE

Faith Gospel Mission

W hile we were living at Chiefland, I was inspired to adopt the name *Faith Gospel Mission* for the ministry I was pursuing and had a sign painted with this logo. I was now a non-denominational Christian evangelist. I still had my car and travel trailer and I went out evangelizing in Florida and Georgia and I would work on whatever jobs were available. I worked in sawmills for .75 cents an hour and was thankful. I began to have wonderful Christian fellowship with the Baptist Purity Church at Salem, Florida and have had fellowship with them since then. I attended some of the summer camp meetings held at Salem, headquarters of the Baptist Purity church, campground and cemetery. A dear Brother in Christ- Luther Turner and his wife Ethel founded this Evangelical movement and in 1952, Brother Turner sold me a canvas tent with the wooden poles for $225.00. A small picture show went out of business up at Vada, Georgia and I was given 35 wooden folding chairs and another preacher friend, Weldon Rentz was also given 35 chairs.

I began to hold Gospel tent meetings in the area along with Brother Barney Young, a member of the Baptist Purity Church who sang, played his guitar and preached. I preached the plain Word of God and played my harmonica with Brother Barney Young accompanying me on his guitar in my tent ministry in Dowling Park, Florida. We had a wonderful series of tent meetings there near the Suwannee

River. The Lord really blessed us in these evangelistic services as we worked on secular jobs in the daytime and preached the Word of God and sang praises at night. I have never sought to be a loner in the Christian ministry. My strongest feeling has always been that God has called the born-again Christian community to work as a team in winning lost souls to Jesus.

After the extended tent meetings at Dowling Park were over, I was offered a job at Branford in another sawmill. I moved my trailer over to Branford and the sawmill owner told me that I could park my trailer in his yard. It so happened that his house was across the street from where Adele was staying. My oldest son Johnny Ray was now about thirteen years old and when he saw our trailer, he immediately came over to visit and he wanted to stay the night. I couldn't say no because I not only wanted him to stay with me but the whole family as well. Adele and her sister came over to our trailer after we had gone to bed and threatened to get the police because John was staying with me. They followed through and an officer from the Branford Police came to investigate but there was nothing he could do about it. Adele contacted her lawyer the next morning and I was summoned back into court and found guilty of contempt of court. The judge sentenced me to twelve months in the Suwannee County jail at Live Oak, Florida. I kindly told the judge that I still loved him and as the jailer led me away, I took Adele's hand and told her that I loved her. She replied that if I had done like I should have, I wouldn't have to go to jail.

The jailer put me in a single cell all alone. Thank God I still had my Bible with me and what a blessing and comfort that was. I knelt on the cell floor and not only prayed for myself but for Adele and our boys, for her family who were opposed to me and for my family members as well. As I was weeping before the Lord, I prayed in earnest that God would put someone else in the cell with me. I wanted someone to talk to. Within a few hours, the jailer brought in another prisoner, a man who had been stealing cows and placed him in the same cell with me. This was comforting. This was on a Saturday night and I don't think this fellow got much sleep because I continued to witness to him of Christ for hours on end. Also, two Christian brothers from the Baptist Purity Church came to visit me in my cell and we had special prayer as we held hands through the cell bars.

Later on that weekend, the jailer came to my cell and told me that if I would pay my wife $60.00 for child support, I would be released. I knew that she already had several thousand dollars in the bank and another $60.00 wouldn't make any economic difference. Even so, I would have given all the money I had to get my family back. The lawyer contacted the judge and on Monday, the next morning, after being in jail for 56 hours, I was released. I went straight to where Adele was living and knocked on the door. When she came to the door, she demanded to know how I had managed to get out of jail. I said, "Honey, they opened the door and I walked out!" I added that I wanted her to go with me to preach the Gospel and she replied that if I would help her wash some clothes, she would go with me. I was accustomed to helping her do washing chores so we got at it and before long, the clothes were clean, dry and folded. We loaded Adele's things and the boys clothing and things into the travel trailer and the next morning, Adele, the boys and I left Branford. We had no planned itinerary but anywhere other than Branford was just fine.

A few days later in the summer of 1952, we arrived in Perry, Florida and parked the trailer. I found out that I could start a prison ministry with the convicts in the Perry Convict Camp. I got a job with the Florida State Highway Department so that I could work more closely with the inmates. I was designated as the prison Chaplain and as such I began conducting evangelistic and Gospel services at the camp. The Captain of the Perry Convict Camp restricted me to having Evangelistic services to twice a month on Sunday mornings. Living and working conditions for inmates were hard at this camp. As a form of punishment, they had a sweatbox measuring 7 feet by 7 feet with a door but no windows and no toilet except for a bucket. An inmate would be put into the sweatbox for a week at a time for any infraction. Many convicts were whipped with a leather strap for infractions of the prison camp rules. This was life in the Florida Chain Gang where even segregation was in effect. The convicts came to confide and trust in me as their Chaplain.

At one point, some convicts informed me that some serious event was to take place. I begged and counseled them to pray to

God for help and to trust Him for a solution to their reprehensible predicament and not do anything to shed blood through violence. The convicts heeded the call of the Holy Spirit and conceded to go on a non-violent, sit-down strike. They requested to only speak with the Florida State Prison Director from the capitol at Tallahassee. The Captain consented and the director came to Perry and each convict was given an opportunity to air his grievance to the state prison director. After all had a chance to speak, the director spoke with the Captain and then the director had a private conference with me in his car. He informed me that changes would be made in the Perry Convict Camp. His assurance was that every convict would get proper medicine and shoes, personal mail, the opportunity to attend Church services every Sunday, that the sweat box was eliminated and that there would be no more whippings. Within a few days, the word was released that dynamite had been planted under the sills of the main barracks ready to blow the guards and buildings to pieces in order to effect an escape. I well remember that the first Sunday after the changes were effected, the same Captain doubled the guard and paced back and forth outside the building where we were having Church services. A much larger number of inmates were attending the services and it made the Captain nervous, but God was in control. Not long afterwards, the Captain was transferred out of Perry. The change in prison policy saved lives and the future of the camp. God intervened in the hearts and lives of those men for their good and I know it was for this very reason that God sent me there. However, none of my own family took any interest in any phase of my Christian ministry.

Relations had improved between Adele and I and we talked about getting a larger travel trailer to live in. Adele agreed to with draw $2,500 dollars from the bank and I put up the remaining amount of $2,800 and we went to Tallahassee and shopped around for a trailer. We purchased a new forty-foot Howard Mansion trailer with $5,300 dollars cash money and it was delivered to us from Tallahassee. This larger trailer gave us the needed room for the family and Adele seemed to be happier. I tried to make her as happy and comfortable as possible under the circumstances of transition from a sedentary, full-time secular business into an Evangelical ministry. At times it seemed that we were successful in getting along and it seemed that things would work out for our marriage and family. I could only continue to pray for God's will to be done in her life and tried to get her to quit smoking cigarettes for her own good but it seemed to be to no avail. She already had me arrested and jailed for no apparent legitimate reason. There were now absolutely no charges against me and other Christians continued to pray for Adele.

After a few months, she decided that she wanted to return to live in Chiefland so I agreed and we bought a half-acre lot on the edge of town from a friend and parked the trailer there. A heavy-drinking man named Gus McCrary lived next door on an acre of land in a small house he had built of rough lumber between drinking sprees. In retrospect, going back to Chiefland was a big mistake for us. Several members of my own family as well as some in-laws, who were vehemently opposed to my Christian ministry and in full sympathy with Adele, effectively wielded some degree of influence over her. I planted a family sized vegetable garden and bought a milk cow. I also bought a horse and a saddle for our oldest son John. I still had my small Gospel tent and began to put it up in Chiefland and around the Williston area to have evangelistic services. Adele refused to have anything to do with these tent meetings. None of my family or in-laws would have anything to do with my evangelistic tent ministry either. I soon discovered that public preaching elicits some interesting as well as strange reactions. The Biblical accounts of the public preaching done by the Apostles Peter and Paul and their helpers prove not only the effectiveness but also the inherent personal risk of danger in such a ministry. History also records the consequences and impact of public preaching conducted by preachers much greater than I such as John the Baptizer, Jesus Christ, John Wesley, George Whitfield, Peter Cartwright, Francis Asbury, Robert Sheffey, and Thomas Griffin. Whenever and wherever men who are dedicated to preaching the Gospel of Jesus Christ declare this message to one and all in a public setting, anything on the spectrum can happen.

One day as I was going into the Chiefland Post Office, I saw something on the sidewalk rolled up in a red cellophane wrapper. I picked it up and unwrapped it. A Gospel tract was inside with the address of the East and West Indies Bible Mission stamped on it. I made contact with this Christian ministry under the leadership of Brother G. T. Bustin. I also met Brother McNabb at their headquarters located at Suwanee Gardens not far from Chiefland. I put up my Gospel tent at this beautiful spot and we had wonderful evangelistic meetings and fellowship. Their doctrine was of the Saved and Sanctified persuasion.

Late in the summer of 1952, after Adele and I moved back to Chiefland, I put up the small Gospel Tent in the front yard where we lived on the northern outskirts of town. I started conducting some meetings under the tent and two women came from Williston to attend one Sunday evening service. I was really impressed by one of these sisters named Mrs. Pearl Carter, wife of Mr. Otis Carter who worked for the Dixie Lilly Milling Company in Williston. Sister Pearl Carter had heard of the little old-fashioned Gospel Tent and being a Holy Spirit filled Christian, came to investigate. She was hungry to hear the Old Time Gospel and that is what the Lord called me to preach. This was the beginning of a friendship and spiritual fellowship that was destined to open many doors in my ministry in Florida, Georgia, and as far north as Pennsylvania. At that time, a Pastor was needed at a small country church named Verbenadale that was located a few miles out from Williston. Of course I felt led of the Holy Spirit to accept the offer of the Pastorate of this small country church. Mr. Otis Carter had a sign made designating this as a Non-Denominational Church with my name on it as Pastor. We continued having Evangelistic services at Verbenadale and also in homes of people I met. We met a lot of good people, most of whom have already gone home to heaven.

About 1953, I made a side trip lasting a month to the Lake Okeechobee and Everglades area in south Florida. I took with me a young Christian man by the name of Osteen to share the message of Jesus Christ among the Seminole Indian people. I worked at a tomato-canning factory as a label machine operator and using conveyors, I helped load cases of canned tomatoes into semi-trailer trucks. Some Seminoles worked at this factory and I was able to witness to them about Christ. Most of the services I conducted were in the Seminole people's homes and under the trees or in the open air in the Everglades area. I found some interest in spiritual things among these dear people and my efforts to minister among the Seminoles was not in vain. My calling and burden was to minister the Word of God among the Native Americans, not as a denominational representative or as an unattached maverick preaching wild fire, but as a Missionary Evangelist sent from the Lord. In the early winter of 1953, Silas, our fourth and last child, was born while we were living in our new trailer at this location. All of our four sons were given names taken from the Bible.

In the summer of 1954, I felt led of the Holy Spirit to leave Chiefland temporarily and take the Faith Gospel Mission tent and my son Jim in our model 1950, Chevrolet pickup truck and head North on US Highway 19. I wanted to conduct some tent meetings in rural South Georgia. We arrived in Pelham, Georgia and stopped at the home of Mrs. Dawson who was the mother of Sister Pearl Carter who we had met previously in Williston, Florida. I told Sister Dawson that I was looking for a place to put up my Gospel tent in order to have some evangelistic meetings. "*Praise God!*" she said, "*You have come to the right place*". I put up the tent on an empty lot next door and Mrs. Dawson's son O. J. had a store across the street from his mother's home. He collected chairs and benches for the tent meeting and donated a new battery for the truck. Some of the Wisham family from the Camilla and Hopeful area of Georgia came out to the meeting and sang and played their musical instruments. These types of rural tent meetings were a demonstration of Southern Gospel music, Christian Ministry and fellowship at its best. This meeting led to friendships that have lasted throughout these many years. I got a job with a plumber and I would work during the day and preach at night. Sister Dawson had another son who lived at Warner Robbins, Georgia and he was in a condition near death. He had heard about me being a non-denominational evangelical minister and wanted me to baptize him. We went up to his community and brought him down to Pelham and on a Sunday afternoon, I baptized him in a fishpond. A month later, O. J. Dawson at Pelham gave me a new pair of shoes so that I could preach his brother's funeral.

I was praying for guidance as to where to go next with the tent and Junior Wisham, Brother Rodney's father, came to me and asked me to come out to the rural community centered around the Father's Home Freewill Baptist Church and preach to the people there. I met Mr. Edgar Wisham, Junior's father and he asked me to put up the tent in his front yard. It was in my nature to work and preach so I went out into the fields to work alongside of these farming people. I hoed in the fields, picked cotton, gathered peanuts and harvested corn with some members of the Wisham family and their neighbors. I labored in everything they had to do except working in the tobacco fields. I felt very strongly then and now that growing tobacco and using it in a way that is detrimental to our health is not for Christians. Bad habits aren't for good people. I have always been a working Preacher and I would advise any Minister to at least get the proper exercise and working at a regular job is a good testimony that is above any reproach.

We had a very good tent revival meeting in this community with the resulting conversions and baptisms of eight people in the Flint River during August of 1954. I baptized Brother Junior Wisham in this swift flowing river near Hopeful, Georgia. At my request to be baptized in running water, he then baptized me in this stream that in some aspects resembles the Jordan River in Israel. It was at this time that I also met Brother Woodrow Sellers and his wife who helped in having two tent meetings in Brinson, Georgia. This chain reaction of meeting so many of God's wonderful children has had a spiritual impact lasting until the present time. I played my harmonicas with the Wisham Singers and the Sellers Family in Georgia, on the radio a few times and in many jails and prisons as we traveled in the United States. Every time we visited with the Wisham family, I was given a place of honor at the head of the table and a place to sleep in the guest room. They had a warm reception for my ministry.

At the tent meetings in the Father's Home and Wisham community, I also met Pastor David Ebersole from the Mennonite Church at Colquitt, Georgia. After hearing me preach, Brother David and others would ask me: "*Where did you learn these doctrines*"? I shared the fact that I had learned the doctrine and theology I held from sincerely studying the Holy Bible. A group of several families from the Lancaster Mennonite Conference came from Pennsylvania in the early 1950's and settled in the area around Colquitt, Georgia.

Their goal as home missionaries was to establish a Mennonite fellowship and to build a Church. Pastor Ebersole had invited me to bring my Gospel tent over to Colquitt and after the meetings at Father's Home Church wound down; I packed up and drove over.

I remember we put up the tent in front of the Piggly Wiggly grocery store, had good services and I became very well acquainted with the Mennonites. During this time, the Ebersole's, Gehman's, Kline's, Longeneckers and other Mennonites as well as the Sellers with the Freewill Baptist Church at Brinson, would invite me into their homes for fellowship and meals. Since most of these Mennonites were farmers, I worked in the fields with these hard working Christians just like one of the family. Later on, when they started construction of the Mennonite Church building, I stayed with Brother David Ebersole and Family and helped work on the building. The exterior cement block walls were laid as high up as the first floor ceiling and one day as we were putting up the ceiling joists and nailing them into place, I was on a joist that was not firmly anchored about nine feet above the cement floor. The joist was moving an inch or more every time another carpenter continued to hammer. The joist slipped off the block wall and I fell head first to the floor. My left hand struck the floor first and my wrist was seriously fractured. Then my head hit the floor and I was knocked unconscious. Brother David Ebersole picked me up and carried me to a car and drove me to the Colquitt Hospital where he watched the doctors set the bones in my left wrist. I wore a cast for about six months and to help the circulation in my arm, I took whirlpool treatments at the Veteran's Administration Hospital in Lake City, Florida. With my arm in a cast, I went to Pennsylvania with Brother David to his sister's wedding. The wedding ceremony of Paul L. Longenecker and Marianna E. Ebersole was truly a marriage ordained in heaven. Having my arm in a cast made it difficult to put on my coat for the occasion. I was very impressed with the Christian convictions, simplicity and sincerity of the Mennonite people. I was treated as one of their family and later on, Pastor Ebersole and other Mennonites made several trips with us to Mexico and helped in our mission work in the state of Coahuila. The Mennonites have been some of my best Christian friends in a fellowship that has lasted for many years.

In the summer of 1956, I took Jim and Paul and went to visit among the Cherokees in North Carolina. We stayed at Big Cove near the city of Cherokee for about a month and this is where I met Pastor John Walkingstick. We would go out on the reservation and round up a pickup truck load of children and have vacation Bible school in an old school building that we were allowed to use. In the evenings, evangelistic services were held for the grownups and children. I played Gospel music on my harmonicas during these meetings. Another Cherokee man by the name of Rattling Leaf helped us in the meetings during our visit. During the day, Jim and Paul along with the Cherokee children would play in the woods and catch rainbow trout by hand in the mountain streams. Our stay among the Cherokee was very rewarding and we had a warm invitation to return.

I continued to evangelize in South Georgia, North and Central Florida and I worked at various trades in order to support my family at Chiefland. Adele would not accompany me to any church unless it was the Southern Baptist Church. I left this religious denomination when I was saved and I had no intention on returning to any organized religious denomination. I would commute back and forth from Florida to Georgia over a period of time conducting a series of tent meetings, jail services, home visitations and Bible studies and public street meetings.

TEN

A Missionary trip to Cuba

In January 1958, I had received an invitation to preach in Guanajay, which was about 35 miles west of Havana, Cuba. In early February of 1958, I made preparations to go to the island of Cuba, which at the time was under attack by Comrade Fidel Castro and his Marxist rebel guerillas. A Mennonite Brother accompanied me on this mission trip and I recorded the trip in my diary.

Thursday, February 13, 1958. "At home and receive telegram from Brother Kauffman. I make plans to go to Williston and Leesburg, on the way to Sarasota and hope to proceed on to Cuba to preach the Gospel. Please dear God, show thy servant thy will in this matter and help me to obey, Amen."

Tuesday the 18th. "At Sarasota, Prepare to go to Cuba, work on sound system, play records and witness to two drunken women and man. Dear Lord: Please save these poor lost souls for Jesus sake."

Wednesday the 19th. "A.M., leave Sarasota with Brother John Kauffman and drive to Key West, spend the night. Thank you Lord for a safe journey. Buy tickets for Cuba. Thank you Lord for keeping us."

Thursday the 20th. "A.M. Board auto ferry and leave Key West. Arrive at Havana, Cuba about 6:30 P.M., then proceed out to Guanajay to Brother Silvano Urra's church and there, Brother Kauffman and I are treated as guests for awhile. Night: I give my testimony at Guanajay and also at another church of Brother Paul Hartman."

Friday the 21st. "Drive back into Havana to see about sound system. The worst traffic I have ever seen. I have the sound system stored for about two weeks. Came by and have dinner at Brother Paul Hartman's, then came back to Guanajay. Thank you Jesus for a safe trip."

Saturday the 22nd. "In Cuba with Brother Silvano Urra. Give out tracts P.M. Drive my car and take a load of people to a funeral. We have supper out on a farm. Old fashioned lamps and supper. Thank you Lord for an opportunity to witness for you on this island."

Sunday the 23rd. "Attend Bible School at Bro. Silvano's church. Play two songs on my harmonica. After dinner, we visit in three homes and witness and give out tracts. Thank you Lord for a real Blessing. Please Dear Lord; help me to preach Thy Word. Night: Begin meetings at Guanajay- I preach on God's Plan in the Ages, Don Smith- Interpreter"

Monday the 24th. "In Guanajay, Cuba with bro. Silvano Urra, give out tracts on the street. Please dear God; help me to speak to these people the plain truth about Bible Holiness. They have heard a social gospel, may there be an awakening. Night: Preach on the subject: The True Church."

Tuesday the 25th. "A.M., Bro. Paul Hartman took us to visit some mission stations south and southeast of Havana. Dear Lord, may the Holy Spirit deal with their hearts and help them to get right with God, that they might preach the pure Gospel. Lord Bless Bro. Hartman. Night: subject- Unfaithful Ministers."
Bro. Hartman- Interpreter."

Wednesday the 26th. "In Guanajay, Cuba with Bro. Silvano Urra. Made visitations in homes. Preach on subject: The Second Coming of Christ. Bro. Paul Hartman did the interpreting. Father please forgive me for being impatient with John Kauffman. Please help me to be more patient and forgive my sin. Help John dear God and use him for your Glory. Amen."

Thursday the 27th. "In Guanajay, Cuba with Bro. Silvano Urra. Went today to a sugar mill but due to the danger of rebel activity, were not allowed to go in. Gave out tracts and witnessed for Jesus. Night: Give testimony and during the message, the lights went out. Thank you Lord for taking care of us. Thank you Lord for a beautiful day."

Friday the 28th. "A.M. visit the United Gospel Mission Station at Cabanas. I met Brother Roy Nelson who seemed to be a real child of God. Found a television set in the home and he said it was his wife who led him to get it. Please Lord; help him to get it out of his house. Afternoon: Visited the San Francisco Dairy Farm. Night subject: The Might of a Minority. Thank you Jesus."

Saturday, March 1, 1958. "A.M., have young people's meeting, about 38 present. Subject: The Three Hebrew Children, Daniel 3rd chapter. Afternoon: I go to Caimito with Silvano and visit several homes and do personal work, give out tracts. Night subject: The Lake of Fire."

Sunday the 2nd. "A.M. Attend the Bible school at Open Bible Church that Bro. Silvano taught. I played my harmonica for the children. Give out tracts. Ate dinner with Estela Freyre and her mother. I received handkerchiefs and socks. Night: I preach on Man-Woman Relationship. The lights went out. Thank you Lord for keeping us safe last night. Close meeting."

Monday the 3rd. "We had prayer with Brother Silvano and Brother Hartman and waved goodbye to them as we passed by. Leave Cuba about 10:00 A.M. and arrived in Key West about 5:00 P.M., then drove on to Sarasota, arrived about 2:00 A.M. Thank you dear Lord for a safe journey."

I had met a Cuban Pastor named Silvano Urra while at the Faith Temple Pentecostal Bible School in St. Petersburg, Florida and my visit to Cuba was based upon his invitation. The few days that I was in Cuba was the first contact I had with the Spanish-speaking people and during my visit in Cuba, I stayed with Pastor Urra and his family in their home. Since I didn't speak any Spanish, I took my battery powered amplifier and turntable, a number of 78-rpm records with Gospel music in Spanish and my metal trumpet speakers. The Cuban customs authorities would not allow me to carry the amplifier and turntable with speakers along with me from the port of Havana so these items were kept there until my departure. I preached in many of the services through an American missionary interpreter named Paul Hartman who was with the Open Bible Church. While on the island of Cuba we experienced a series of very good evangelistic meetings in several churches and were welcomed into several homes. My visit in Havana was unforgettable especially in dealing with the city streets and traffic. I learned very quickly through experience how to negotiate most intersections. If you heard a horn blow you'd better stop since the other driver that honked his horn first had the right of way and was going on through the crossing. Apparently, red traffic signal lights didn't mean much there at that time.

During the short time we visited in Pastor- Silvano Urra's home, Brother Kauffman and I had to sleep in the same bed. He always wanted to pull the covers up over his head in spite of the absence of mosquitoes in the home and as customary; I wanted to have the covers under my chin. This created something of a problem with no apparent solution. Also, in my preaching, I preached a strong non-sectarian message. Brother Kauffman was a member of the Mennonite Church and thought that I was speaking directly against his church organization. The Apostle Paul said in 1 Corinthians, 3rd chapter, that "*whereas there are divisions, you are yet carnal*". All religious denominations are man-made. The irony of it all at the time was that the Communists were as much or more dedicated to violent revolution in Cuba as we Christians were to evangelizing the Cubans. It seems that the Marxists were more unified in purpose than the Christians were. There is only one True Church composed of all Born-Again, faithful Christians and that is the only one that is going to be with the Lord in the Rapture or second-coming of Christ. It was over this conflict that I had to shorten my missionary trip to Cuba. In spite of the temporal conflict, we were really blessed of the Lord and would have enjoyed staying for a longer period of time.

I also went out into the countryside and observed the sugar cane fields and workers. All of the sugar cane was harvested by hand labor using machetes to cut the stalks, gathered and loaded onto oxcarts and transported to the refineries. During this time, Fidel Castro and the Communist rebels were fighting in the hills and jungles of Cuba against the corrupt government of President Fulgencio Batista. One night, we came to a roadblock manned by two soldiers. They shined their flashlights into the car and checked us over thoroughly. For a while it appeared that they were uncertain as to what to do with us. After some discussion among themselves, one of the soldiers came over to the car and tapped twice in rapid succession on the hood saying: *"Pase"*, meaning to proceed. People were getting killed in various parts of Cuba due to the anti-Batista guerrilla warfare. We heard that an American woman had been stopped at a roadblock and she had reached into her purse for a lipstick. The trigger-happy soldiers apparently thought she was going for a gun and shot her in the head.

During some of the church services, the electric lights went off all over town. Twice, the Communist rebels in our area would short-circuit the power lines by taking a length of chain, tie a rope on one end and throw the chain over some electric lines, create a short circuit and blow out the transformers. We lit kerosene lamps and continued on with the church services. Not long after my visit in Cuba, the darkness of the iron curtain descended on the beautiful island and the light of the Gospel was dimmed but not extinguished.

I enjoyed my short missionary visit to the country of Cuba and I would like to return someday. Cuba is a beautiful country and it is unfortunate that the wonderful people on this beautiful Caribbean island have been ruled for so long by a ruthless, atheist, Communist dictator. I never heard from Pastor Silvano Urra after visiting in

Cuba and I hope and pray that Pastor Urra and his family survived the persecution and genocide committed by Marxists against the Christians there.

ELEVEN

Pastorate and Evangelism

W e returned to the United States and I went back to Chiefland to see my family. I would work the family sized garden and attend to chores around the house that needed to be done. Of course, I had no welcome from anyone when I came back home from Cuba and typically, no plaudits for preaching even in a foreign country from any of my family.

It wasn't very long before I was back in Leesburg, Florida working with Brother Mosley, preaching and ministering in and out of churches in that part of the country. I kept the family supplied with the food, clothing and shelter they needed. I will say they didn't get every little thing they wanted but all the necessary items were well supplied. I tried to be a witness for Jesus Christ everywhere I went.

On Thursday, April 10, 1958, Brother Weldon Rentz and I got permission from the Sheriff to use the Baker County Courthouse in Newton, Georgia for a Gospel meeting. We had Brother Woodrow and his wife, Sister Edna Sellers from Brinson, Georgia to provide the Gospel music for the services. We used the judge's stand as the pulpit. Some of the Mennonites came out to the meeting from Colquitt and we all had a wonderful time of Christian fellowship and community outreach during the nine days of meeting in the Baker County courthouse.

My diary entries for this time period read:

Monday, April 14, 1958. "A.M. visitation, P.M. Sweep out the court-room and prepare for meetings, then broadcast. Night: Begin meetings in Baker County Courthouse in Newton, Georgia with Brother Rentz. I speak on the subject of God's Plan in the Ages."

Tuesday the 15th. "Continue Gospel meetings in the courtroom, about 50 present and some came from a far distance. The Sellers played and sang and Brother Longenecker led a testimony meeting. I preached on the subject: The Fall of man, 3rd chapter of Genesis."

Wednesday the 16th. "Continue Gospel meeting, about 40 present, I preach on the subject: "SIN." Thank you Lord for the anointing of Thy Holy Spirit. May souls be saved is our prayer."

Thursday the 17th. "Brother Rentz preached, about 30 present."

Friday the 18th. "Give testimony of my conversion, about 30 present."

Saturday the 19th. "A.M. I help Brother Rentz plow his garden, cut the boys hair. P.M. We have a street meeting in Newton; subject: "HELL"- Luke 16:19, 31 Good attendance. Night: Brother Longenecker spoke at meeting in the courthouse. Praise God for one soul that came to the altar."

Sunday the 20th. "P.M. I visited a man dying with cancer and explained the way to heaven. He was hard to convince."

Monday the 21st. "Gospel meeting, about 9 present. Subject: "The Great Tribulation."

Tuesday the 22nd. Close meeting at courthouse, about 30 present. Subject: Religion- true or false."

I returned home to Chiefland after visiting around with some of the Christian Believers in South Georgia and at Salem, Florida. I worked on different jobs and took care of things at home. I tried to read the Bible to the boys and endeavored to take them to church with me. I was still pastoring the Verbenadale Non-Denominational Church when I was at home. Adele would still have no part in my ministry and she didn't encourage the boys to accompany me to preach or even to go to church. I had no encouragement whatsoever from any one of my in-laws or from my family to carry on the Christian ministry that God had definitely called me into. In fact, all members of the family were very much opposed to any notion of me conducting a ministry of any kind, especially in or near Chiefland.

I had permanently seceded from the Southern Baptist Church and my Dad told me: "*If you would just come back into the church and be one of us, everything would be all right*". This was something I just could not do. I'm not sure where my Dad got the belief but he and I once had a heated discussion about actually knowing that we were saved. He would become very irritated when I would mention anything about being Born-Again. He stated: "*We cannot know whether we are saved until the moment that we die, then we would know if we were going to heaven or not.*" Poppa was adamant with me about we couldn't know in this life concerning the assurance or knowledge of our salvation. I could only disagree. On one occasion, he became so implacably upset with me over a theological discussion that he bluntly ordered me to leave his property. The Word of God simply declares: "*These things have I written unto you that believe on the name of the Son of God; that ye may know that ye have eternal life, and that ye may believe on the name of the Son of God*". (1 John 5:13) I believed then and now concerning the conditions for God's Holy Spirit being manifested and continuing in a visible body of Believers. The evidence is found in the Word of God and throughout the general history of the church and Rev. Thomas Griffin summarizes this truth very well. "*If our people* (Methodists) *are not faithful, God will raise up another sect— for He will have a people.*" (Thomas Griffin, p. 210) Sometimes, individuals and groups do grieve the Holy Spirit and His presence departs. God will only have a people who will implicitly trust and obey his Word. This truth applies to any individual, denomination, group or organization and God rejects all apostasy.

Viewing the past in retrospect, I was apparently perceived as some sort of an ignorant, maverick preacher lacking in formal theological education, a troublemaker and an embarrassment to some of the family. Consequently, I had very little spiritual fellowship with any of my family. Regardless of where I put up my Gospel tent to have meetings or if I conducted any street meetings, none of my family ever came out to visit or participate in them. As a non-denominational evangelist, I was avoided like the bubonic plague. In spite of the contrary feeling, I thought that things were going pretty well in the ministry. Christian fellowship across some denominational lines was getting warmer and souls were being saved and blessed in the evangelistic meetings. Through the combined efforts of my outreach ministry and other believers helping me, God was moving in the hearts and lives of people in several communities in North Carolina, North and Central Florida, South Georgia and even in Cuba. For me, this was a period of intense evangelistic outreach and interdenominational fellowship especially in Florida and Georgia and I had no premonition or warning of what was about to happen to me. No one gave me any adumbration or hint of the ferocious storm about to break.

TWELVE

Chattahoochee to Gulf Port— A Spiritual Odyssey

Historical legend has it that the Lower Creek Indian people referred to a Creek village as "Chatu-huchi," apparently located along the river that later became known as the Chattahoochee. This river plays an important geographical role in Georgia, Alabama and Florida. The river has a rich physical and cultural history, stretching from prehistory through early pioneer settlement to the present day. Rev. Thomas Griffin crossed over and traveled upon the Chattahoochee River several times in his missionary journeys. Some Civil War boats lie rotting in its murky waters while others are preserved in museums along its banks. The bustle of modern society, the hum of bass fishing boats, the skirl of Celtic pipes, and the excitement of Boy Scout jamborees and Girl Scout camps have replaced the sounds of Indigenous chants and throbbing drums along the river's length. Throughout many centuries, the adversity of periodic flooding has enriched farmlands along its floodplains and delta on the gulf coast.

The ancient Creek Indian term Chatu-huchi literally means a marked rock that we call a petroglyph. In a Biblical context, Jesus Christ the Messiah and rock of our salvation, is in a spiritual sense, our "Chatu-huchi" or marked rock. "He *hath no form or comeliness, there is no beauty that we should desire him… he was wounded for our transgressions, he was bruised for our iniquities.*" (Isaiah 53) In spite of social adversity and human frailty, my spiritual life was enriched by the unique experience I had in the place called Chattahoochee. The second and fifth stanzas of a poem called The Song of the Chattahoochee seem to have a special meaning in relation to my experience on a bank of this mysterious river.

> Out of the hills of Habersham, down the valleys of Hall,
> I hurry amain to reach the plain, run the rapid and leap the fall...
> The rushes cried Abide, abide, the willful waterweeds held me thrall,
> the laving laurel turned my tide, the ferns and the fondling grass said stay, the dewberry dipped for to work delay, and the little reeds sighed Abide, abide. But oh, not the hills of Habersham, and oh, not the valleys of Hall,
> Avail: I am fain for to water the plain, Downward the voices of duty call—
> Downward, to toil and be mixed with the main, the dry fields burn, and the mills are to turn, and a myriad flowers mortally yearn, And the lordly main from beyond the plain, calls o'er the hills of Habersham, Calls through the valleys of Hall. (Sidney C. Lanier, 1842—1881, Public Domain)

But life is not always so idyllic along the Chattahoochee River in Florida. Early on the morning of May 9, 1958, I was working with my youngest son Silas, hoeing the grass and weeds out of our family garden near Chiefland. With no warning, a Levy County Sheriff's car arrived at our house and out stepped one of the deputy sheriff's officers. He came walking over to me and introduced himself as Officer Doty Drummond. I knew him quite well as we had attended high school together in Chiefland. He plainly stated that I had to accompany him to the county seat of Bronson. I asked him what was the matter and he said that the county judge would explain it to me. At that time, there were no Miranda Rights in existence.

Deputy Drummond allowed me to go into the house to change clothes and to get my Bible. Adele was sitting on the bed and acted like she didn't know anything about what was happening. She demanded some money for groceries, which I gave to her. I had been keeping a personal diary of important daily events in 1958, and this is the primary source record.

Friday, May 9, 1958. "At about 9:00 A.M., while working in the family garden, I was arrested by Deputy Drummond and carried to Bronson and put in the Levy County Jail. Absolutely no charges, he told me I would see the Judge, not so."

Saturday the 10th. "In solitary confinement in the Bronson jail."

Sunday the 11th. "In Bronson jail, Brother Fred Stevens came and preached to us prisoners. Afternoon, Iree brought me some cake."

Monday the 12th. "In Bronson jail, no charges. I didn't get to talk with the county judge like they said."

Tuesday the 13th. "In Bronson jail."

Wednesday the 14th. "In Bronson jail."

Thursday the 15th. "In Bronson jail, Dr. Fernal and Dr. Jordan from Trenton came to ask me questions."

Friday the 16th. "In Bronson jail."

Saturday the 17th. "In Bronson jail, waiting to be sent to Chattahoochee."

Sunday the 18th. "In Bronson, Levy County, Florida- jail."

Monday the 19th. "Early in the morning, two deputies took me to Chattahoochee to the receiving ward. They took my clothes and some of my money and put me on a locked ward."

The deputy took me to the courthouse in Bronson and without being able to speak with the county judge, a lawyer or anyone else, he turned me over to the jailer and I was placed in a cell of solitary confinement. I was never read any rights or given any warnings since the historic Miranda case was still over five years away from becoming a precedent and the established rule of law. Consequently, I was not informed as to why I was being detained and incarcerated. I never was allowed the chance to even speak to the judge. Perhaps I was as unimportant as dust swept under a rug.

By virtue of the way my case was handled, it appears that the State of Florida violated my Constitutional rights, especially the 14th Amendment which reads: Section 1- *"All persons born or naturalized in the United States, and subject to the jurisdiction thereof, are citizens of the United States and of the State wherein they reside. No State shall make or enforce any law which shall abridge the privileges or immunities of citizens of the United States; nor shall any State deprive any person of life, liberty or property, without due process of law; nor deny to any person within its jurisdiction the equal protection of the laws"*. The 14th Amendment was passed by the United States Congress on June 13, 1866, and ratified on July 9, 1868. The 14th Amendment fully applied to cases such as mine for a full ninety years before I was deprived of my liberty and my life put at risk on the basis of a discriminatory mis-diagnosis made by a biased and unqualified ad hoc panel. I was denied these rights: The free exercise of religion, to be secure against unreasonable seizure, a warrant for arrest, the right of a judicial hearing, the right to a speedy and public trial, the right to be informed as to the nature and cause of the accusations against me, the right to confront my accusers, the provision of legal counsel for defense, protection from cruel and unusual punishment, and I was denied representation in government by virtue of the summary deprivation of my citizenship. (Amendments-1, 4, 5, 6, 8 & 14; Sect. 2)

I was kept in the Levy County jail for a total of nine and a half days wondering what was going on. I was in solitary confinement there for about seven days. I am still curious as to what empirical evidence justified my arrest and incarceration for nine and one-half days in a county jail with no hearing or formal charges. I hadn't "lost it" and shot up the neighborhood, I had not physically attacked or assaulted any one, I hadn't made any kind of threats toward any one, I had no nervous ticks or anxiety attacks and I wasn't foaming at the mouth, howling at the moon or biting people with my dentures. I was never charged with brawling or public drunkenness and had never committed any acts of arson, sedition or treason. I was not incoherent in speech or catatonic; I wasn't somnambulant or chewing my tongue. I had never used mind-altering drugs and wasn't having flashbacks. I was not tuning in to some oddball counter-cultural philosophy, turning on to illicit drugs and dropping out of mainstream society. I never desecrated the flag of the United States or burned any draft cards, and I never rioted or firebombed any government buildings in the spirit of violent revolution. No one accused me of lewd behavior in public, I was not a ragamuffin homeless person mumbling and gesticulating while pushing a shopping cart stuffed with my earthly possessions along city streets, and I was never seen trying to jump off tall buildings and bridges. I have no record of depression or Post-Traumatic Stress Disorder. All that I lost in World War Two were all of my teeth, not even hardly approaching sufficient a trauma to develop some type of phrenia over. I never manifested any symptoms of Schizophrenia such as alogia, anhedonia, avolition, or polydipsia. All of my reflexes were completely normal with no exotic irregularities and I had no exhaustion or loss of motor ataxia. I definitely wasn't suicidal; quite on the contrary, I was on the upward way gaining new heights every day with Jesus Christ my Lord. The experience of having hallucinations was as foreign to me as incarceration in solitary confinement which at the time definitely was not a hallucination. So, what possible crime was I "guilty" of to be arrested, incarcerated and committed to an insane asylum in the manner I was treated?

While I was there, a preacher named Fred Stephens came to conduct church services in the jail on Sundays. I had met Brother Stephens while I was pastoring at Verbenadale Church. All the prisoners who wanted to be in the church service were put into a large cell. I took a songbook and really sang my heart out. Brother Fred Stephens was an acquaintance of mine but he didn't understand why

I was in the county jail. During my stay at Bronson, my oldest sister Iree came to visit and brought me some cake.

After about a week, our family physician, Dr. Fernal, accompanied by another medical doctor, came to visit me in the jail. They came into the cell, greeted me and sat down. All they did was to ask a singular question about what had happened to me. I explained that what had happened to me was the Biblical experience of Salvation by Grace through Faith. I gave them my testimony in detail of the how and why of my conversion to Jesus Christ eight years previous and the pursuant Christian ministry that God had called me into. I told the two physicians of how the Lord had baptized me with the Holy Ghost and fire and that aspiring to be an Evangelical Missionary, I wanted to preach the Gospel according to the will of God. The two doctors listened very carefully and without any comment, got up and left.

The certified copy of Florida state form XL-10 that I have, reads that an Inquisition of Incompetence was issued by the Court of the County Judge of Levy County, Florida on May 9, 1958. The court appointed committee to inquire into my mental competency was composed of Harry Jordan, M.D., Fernal, M.D., and Willie Green-Clerk of the Levy County Court. I would like to explain a little more in detail about the two doctors who visited me in the Levy County Jail. Their visit was a lawful requirement relevant to the commitment of any person to the state hospital. It appears that I was detained the nine days in the Levy County Jail until a bed became available for me in the Florida State Hospital at Chattahoochee. The doctors had to at least go through a pretense of examining me in order to determine whether I would be sent on as a patient to Chattahoochee or not. It was decided by Dr. Jordan, our family doctor from Trenton, and Dr. Fernal, that I was to be sent on to Chattahoochee. I was held in the Levy County Jail without being told of the actual plans and timetable relevant to my case until the last night that I was there.

The following morning, I was accompanied by two sheriff's deputies and sat in the back seat of the sheriff's car. I was taken to the Florida State Hospital at Chattahoochee, up near the Florida and Georgia line. It was about noon when we arrived at the receiving ward. I was involuntarily committed into the maelstrom of a system that channeled an endless supply of "patients" into a repository of human crumbs. Chattahoochee was the ultimate in the application of social anathema and ostracism. In 1957, alone, one county in Florida sent three-hundred people to Chattahoochee. (Donaldson, p. 111) In the late 1950's, the fee system for such transfers of humans from the free world to Chattahoochee was thirty-five dollars per head, paid in full by the state taxpayers and bolstering the budgets of many county sheriff's departments. (Donaldson, p. 115) Only God and the guilty know what other agencies and departments benefited in like manner. It was a local pork barrel fed by the human crumbs.

It seems that during the time I was held at Chattahoochee, this egregious system created a comfortable level of job security for certain psychiatrists and support staff. It is no secret that some pawky psychiatrists have the propensity to slant their official finding toward the side that employs them. In many fields of employment when money talks the money grubbers always listen. It is beyond any element of doubt that many "patients" were railroaded into Chattahoochee, classified as being ill with any aspect of a wide range of real or imagined mental disorders, mixed in with the general population of those people who were legitimately insane and the criminal element, all of whom were maintained on a diet of institutional food, oftentimes of dubious quality, most patients being administered any number of "treatments" which were at best spurious for an undetermined number, thereby establishing a guaranteed income for the elitist medical staff. The almost inescapable habitat of Chattahoochee generously supplied all the factors required for the existence of a niche industry for an unknown number of low to high-level private and state employees. Only God and the guilty ones know how long this local pork-barrel system was carried on the backs of the taxpayers.

An editorial entitled: Society's Warehouses, concerning the tragic case of Mr. Kenneth Donaldson, was published on November 12, 1974, in the New York Times. It says: *"There are dark corners in America where people are trampled, broken and forgotten. The saddest of these- and the most demeaning to our society-are those institutions, paid for and run by the public, where people are stashed away for the safety and convenience of the rest of us and then left to rot untouched by the collective conscience of the community.*

Attica and Soledad turned flickering attention toward the prisons; but few have cared to look at those huddled in the rotten crannies of America's mental institutions. Last month the Supreme Court gave some hope that it will use the powerful lever of the Fourteenth Amendment to pry open doors that an enlightened citizenry should have forced open years ago. It took the case of a man named Kenneth Donaldson, who after civil commitment, spent fifteen years in a Florida State Hospital. When he was committed, the judge told Mr. Donaldson that he was being sent away for "a few weeks" to "take some of this new medication." Mr. Donaldson received no medication and no treatment, and finally, in 1971, he filed suit for his freedom and for damages. During his stay in the hospital, Mr. Donaldson's home was a locked room with 60 beds jammed side by side. At least a third of the residents of that room were deemed criminally insane. Mr. Donaldson's "treatment" was described by his doctors as a "milieu therapy"—that is, being hospitalized with other mental patients. Kenneth Donaldson is now out and thanks to the courts and the Fourteenth Amendment, he may also receive some recompense for his fifteen years. But there are tens of thousands of Kenneth Donaldsons both out of sight and out of mind. The Fourteenth Amendment can't operate as a civilizing influence for all of them. Only the decent impulses of society can do that". (Copyright 1974, by The New York Times Co. -Reprinted with permission)

Generally, the path of life is strewn with iniquities as well as with inequities and the truth is that we are all created equal by God but we aren't all treated as equal by some of our peers. In spite of the fact that the Declaration of Independence states: *"We hold these truths to be self-evident, that all men are created equal; that they are endowed by their Creator with inherent and inalienable rights; that among these, are life, liberty, and the pursuit of happiness; that to secure these rights, governments are instituted among men, deriving their just powers from the consent of the governed"*, oftentimes our fellow man treats us according to quite another standard.

During the American War Between the States, President-Abraham Lincoln affirmed the concept of inalienable Constitutional equality in his Gettysburg Address: *"Four-score and seven years ago, our fathers brought forth upon this continent a new nation, conceived in liberty and dedicated to the proposition that all men are created equal*". The fact that I was involuntarily committed to an insane asylum with no *Mens rea* present (meaning wrongful state of mind, i.e. the state of mind indicating culpability which is required by lawful statute as an element of a crime) (www.law.cornell.edu/wex/index.php/Mens_rea) and no record or manifestation of *Actus rea* (an act by the defendant, which results in a prohibited harm to society which is the other required element of a crime needed to convict), evidences that my physical and mental well-being were placed in jeopardy, my liberty was completely deprived, and my pursuit of happiness evaporated with the drying of the signatory ink on the official forms of Inquisition of Incompetency. (www.law.cornell.edu/wex/index.php/Actus_rea)

Said in another way: 1. Mental state (*mens rea*), 2.- Physical act (one component of *actus rea*) and; 3. Social harm (another component of *actus rea*). (http://tech.clayton.edu) The criminal act is a combination of these elements. I can truthfully declare before God and man that I have never perpetrated any crime against anyone nor have I committed any prohibited harm to society after my genuine conversion to Christianity.

The parody of injustice sometimes found in societies is presented very clearly in the novel titled Animal Farm. The "lower" and "undesirable" animals had value only in how they could best serve the interests of the ruling class of animals. This kind of utilitarianism has existed in America and across the globe and is now the apparent neo-liberal standard by which human life is judged in America. Human embryonic stem cell (*HESC*) research is a case in point since aborted human embryos are destroyed by dissection in order to obtain usable cells. In some of America's so-called scientific laboratories, tiny aborted human beings at the earliest stages of life are sacrificed in impeccable and sterile environments through Dr. Mengele-like experiments because their fetal lives and tissues have been deemed valuable only in how they can best serve the economic interests of certain corporate entities in the name of progressive modern medical science. The results of fetal stem cell research has promised some medical benefits to the rest of humanity but the real value of these aborted fetuses is measured in dollars in terms of corporate profits.

The commercial use of HESC raises many legitimate moral questions, generates concerns about success rates, it stimulates drug sales, and it introduces the bizarre Jekyl / Hyde specter of chimeras or the mixing of animal and human species. God defends the rights of human embryos since God recognizes the status and validity of human life from conception. Human life has sanctity based on its creation by God. *"The Word of the Lord... Before I formed thee in the belly I knew thee; and before thou camest forth out of the womb I sanctified thee."* (Jeremiah 1:4, 5) *"Behold, I was shapen in iniquity; and in sin did my mother conceive me."* (Psalm 51:5) *"The Lord himself shall give you a sign; a virgin shall conceive, and bear a son, and shall call his name Immanuel."* (Isaiah 7:14) The Ten Commandments plainly state: *"Thou shalt not kill."* (Exodus 20:13 and Deut. 5:17) The Word of God says that everything shall be established in the mouths of three or four witnesses and among the plethora of eyewitnesses of the eternal truth concerning the sanctity of human life are these four Patriarchs and Prophets: Moses, Jeremiah, Elijah, and Isaiah.

Contrasted with human embryonic stem cell research is the more acceptable realm of human adult stem cell research including certain types of transplants. Its successful applications include plasticity, it is much less controversial and it is profitable in various ways to individuals and medical science. It doesn't matter so much what any president or the federal or state governments decide about HESC, what does God think, feel and say about this specific issue? This is a moral and spiritual issue and a power much higher than the politicians and scientists will ultimately decide on judgment. On the other end of life's spectrum, we see a similar utilitarian philosophy that withholds medical treatments from the elderly or to certain "brain-dead" patients simply because it is deemed they just aren't worth the expenditure of resources that could go to someone with a longer life expectancy. It appears that no one in the secular world is asking God for His perspective about mere fickle men playing god while tinkering around with the priceless human life that our Omnipotent God purposefully created.

The universal command of Jesus Christ to: *"Love thy neighbor as thyself"*, applies to the entire spectrum of all humans. God's direc-

112

tive concerns all human life from conception, in the womb, on the street, in asylums and extends to the infirm, handicapped and aged. Unfortunately, the Word of God is completely ignored by the neo-liberal, secular-humanists. Some pseudo-liberal Orwellian philosophies inherent within some religions in America seem to paraphrase a spiritualized socio-political concept presented in Animal Farm: *"All Preachers are created equal but some Preachers are created more equal than others"*. According to the Constitution of These United States, we all have human rights, civil rights and legal rights but in reality, some people seem to have or exercise more rights than others in terms of legal positivism, denominational privilege and / or through socio-economic and political aristocracies.

In retrospect, I must have put certain aspects of the United States Constitution and some theories of political science to the ultimate test through preaching the Gospel in public places since the response was similar in effect as those public scenes of Jesus, John the Baptizer, the Apostles, Wesley, Whitfield and many others. Throughout Christian history, the world's typical response to prolonged, serious public preaching of God's Word oftentimes involves gnashing, false accusations and verbal hostility, stonings, beatings, rendings, banishment, blasphemy and libel, mob violence, incarceration and even murder perpetrated upon the Gospel messenger. The cowards of the world cannot hit God to silence Him so they almost invariably, in some way or another, attack the messenger of God.

I know some of the history of Dr. Fernal, M.D. (General Practitioner). I can say that in spite of the fact that he was our local family doctor, he was not even remotely qualified to be a psychiatric authority to question or to judge anyone's mental competency since he had previously blown off his own left hand by illegally dynamiting fish on the Suwannee River. An older brother was a Deacon in the local Baptist church and my brother and the doctor along with their wives were all close-knit workers in the same denominational church making them religious bosom buddies. It just so happened that later on, a niece was married to the doctor's son. When I left their church, they all in fact became very upset with me over the matter and when the time came to make a decision in my case, Dr. Fernal, very likely under some sociological pressure or influenced by the compunction of close family and religious ties, signed the inquisition papers for me to be committed to the infamous Florida State Hospital at Chattahoochee. It seems that someone had the desire to have me put out of sight and out of mind for good like dust swept under the rug. Later on, a sister-in-law told me in harsh terms that she knew who had sent me to Chattahoochee but that she wasn't going to inform me as to whom it was. The "secret" hasn't been one of absolute confidence since the records pertinent to the case are in the Florida State Archives and are public knowledge.

I have prayed to God to help me not to harbor any ill feeling in my heart against any one. My earnest prayer has always been for everyone involved in this feudal, sordid and mercenary family affair to be saved by the Grace of God and to make sure that heaven is to be their eternal home. As for Dr. Jordan and court clerk Green, I don't know much about their lifestyles but ponder their motive and I question their professional judgment. If a mental condition such as schizophrenia, associated with paranoia and hallucinations, is judged to be chronic, then such a condition would certainly have lasted much longer than from May 9, 1958, to August 26, 1958, when the panel of examining doctors declared that I was not insane. The dictum of the original Inquisition Committee categorically declared: *"We determine that Jack R. Griffin is incompetent, the apparent cause being schizophrenia, the same is chronic, the particular hallucinations are some paranoia, his propensities are fight, his age is 43, and he does not require mechanical restraints to prevent him from self-injury or violence to others. He is destitute and is eligible to be committed as such"*. Some psychiatrists believe that an ambiguous combination of factors such as being born male, being born in the wintertime and being born in an industrialized country are viable contributors to the development of schizophrenia. I suppose that means I was doomed from birth since all these factors fit me to a "T". Be that as it may, it should be noted that the definition of the term chronic indicates that a diagnosed disease would linger, be of long duration and likely be recurring and possibly fatal.

Someone truly afflicted with chronic schizophrenia would very likely be in an insane asylum or medical institution for a much, much longer time than the three months and eight days that I was actually in Chattahoochee under strict observation all the while. In reality, I was not taking any medicines or drugs, not receiving electric shock or insulin treatments and certainly not undergoing any lobotomies to change or cure my purported condition of chronic schizophrenia. It is readily apparent that I must not have been afflicted with chronic schizophrenia or any other form of mental incompetency or insanity from the beginning since I never had any kind of treatment and the alleged chronic condition I was judged to have was extremely short-lived. The card for my admission into Chattahoochee states that the person who had me committed was my wife and that she left before signing the admission papers. This evidences that the desire to dump me into Chattahoochee was so acute that even the papers were left unsigned in the hasty exit. Consequently, the admission card bears the information that her attorney, C. Edwards, signed the admission papers, in essence doing the dirty work he was paid to do with my own money.

Many of the buildings for the Florida State Hospital are quite old. The original complex of buildings imposed upon the rolling red clay hills and piney woods of northern Florida in 1832, was originally a pioneer armory created for the defense of the Florida frontier. Not long before I was committed, the status of the institution had been changed from asylum to state hospital but no stranger would realize that it had in fact become a glorified prison with a significant population of inmates held against their will. The screens on the windows were made of almost impenetrable spring steel.

As we entered the receiving ward, I was led to the same desk that all patients are led to upon entering. The sheriff's deputies gave the nurse my records, signed some papers and left. I was admitted to my new home on May 19, 1958, as patient # A-27770, and I had no idea as to how long I would be in Chattahoochee. I was taken to a back room for a bath, given institutional clothing after my civilian clothing was taken away, and some of my money was taken from me. I had carefully hidden some of my money in my Bible and I quickly found out that almost none of the staff or inmates had much to do with the Holy Bible and that this was the safest place to keep one's money. The institutional pajamas, bathrobe and slippers were what we wore all the time. Of course, I had no liberty or a way to go to any church services while I was there.

Every one that came in was placed in a locked ward for the initial period of two weeks. Every inmate was given daily doses of a powerful tranquilizer containing 400 milligrams of the potent drug-Thorazine. We had to stand in front of the nurse administering the tablet three times daily. I took the Thorazine tablets for three days until I became so constipated that I could hardly go to the bathroom. I got down on my knees and prayed to my Heavenly Father and asked Him what I was to do in this situation. I was getting deathly sick on my stomach. My Heavenly Father plainly impressed upon me to simply not swallow the tablets and that He would help me to flush the drugs down the toilet without anyone noticing me. God doesn't want us to use mind-altering drugs that confuse us or that alter reality. The Almighty has a better way than for us to use such drugs. The Holy Spirit of God is the key to our happiness and guarantees us mental soundness. I obeyed the Lord and in spite of the careful observations of the nurses, no one ever saw or knew of how I successfully avoided swallowing the drug tablets but rather allowed the institutional toilet to take the drugs instead. I recovered quickly from the stuporous and lethargic effects of the Thorazine and after the first two weeks were past, I was allowed to go outside during the daylight hours. I would play ball with some of the others, take brisk walks and I tried to keep up a regular exercise regimen. I helped to sweep and mop the floors and maintained a perfect record all the while I was at Chattahoochee.

The truth of the matter is that there were some really sick people at the Florida State Hospital. There were several lunatic persons on the ward who were physically dangerous and they would walk up and hit you from behind. I had to keep a sharp watch all around myself in order to avoid any violent attacks upon my person. I knew very quickly after arriving in Chattahoochee that I did not belong in an institution where a number of patients defecated in their clothing and on the floor, where patients would scream and holler for many hours at a time, where some women were locked in rooms, clad in straight jackets, and some staff would abuse and prey upon defenseless patients in many ways.

Pretty soon, I was moved to an open ward that was locked only at night. We had better company on this ward and I got a job in the kitchen helping to serve the meals. I got all I wanted to eat and some other privileges and I thanked God for all my blessings. After 30-days, the medical staff wrote my wife a letter telling her that if she would come to Chattahoochee they wanted a conference with her regarding our future plans. It was readily apparent that the psychiatrists were not finding any aberrant behavior in me during their observations and examinations. I firmly believe that I would have been discharged at that time if my wife had of come to Chattahoochee but she refused. Another inmate, Kenneth Donaldson, was in Chattahoochee while I was there. He was confined against his will in this state hospital for fifteen years and eventually sued the State of Florida and the Superintendent of Chattahoochee to regain his freedom. He also had done nothing dangerous or criminal but nevertheless, was held by Chattahoochee Superintendent Dr. J. B. O'Connor: "for care, maintenance, and treatment". In reality, Kenneth Donaldson and many other innocent men and women held against their will at Chattahoochee and elsewhere, were not only slam-dunked into an institution but also intentionally and maliciously deprived of their constitutional right to liberty; sometimes for years. We were lied to in that the hospital staff told us that we had to be signed out by a relative. Mr. Donaldson's trial showed clear evidence that: *"the hospital staff had the power to release a patient, not dangerous to himself or others, even if he remained mentally ill and had been lawfully committed. Despite many requests, Dr. O'Connor refused to allow that power to be exercised. This rule was apparently of O'Connor's own making. Donaldson's confinement was a simple regime of enforced custodial care, not a program designed to alleviate or cure his supposed illness"*. (U.S. Supreme Court- O'Connor- vs – Donaldson, 422 U.S. 563 (1975) Sect. 1, p. 3, 4) My case was not dramatically different but the overall length of my confinement was. Some of us survived Chattahoochee in spite of all odds to the contrary.

THIRTEEN

Jesus Loves Me

God called me to be an Evangelist and as the Apostle affirms in the divinely inspired Word of God in First Corinthians chapter nine, verse sixteen; *"Woe is me if I preach not the Gospel"*. In the Florida State Hospital at Chattahoochee, Florida, a few other believers and I were not allowed to give an open witness for Jesus Christ. Christianity, I'm talking about true Christianity, and insanity is considered by many unbelievers to be on the same level. The world in general doesn't recognize a real Born-Again, Holy Spirit filled Christian believer. Oftentimes it is thought that he or she might have had a nervous breakdown or flipped out and behaves irrationally. This is the reason why they wanted to administer the Thorazine drug to me at Chattahoochee. It was purportedly to calm my nerves, which were completely intact and not frayed or broken. Supposedly, persons afflicted by Schizophrenia hear voices; have hallucinations and other exotic mental experiences. If I "hear" the Word of God through fervent prayer or through serious Biblical research and analysis with the perfectly legal objective of obeying the Word of God, am I or any other Bible student of the Berean category- insane? How and why should I lose my mind, reason or sanity when having the mind of Christ is a process of spiritual renewal and restoration of body, mind and soul? Having a close spiritual relationship with my Creator and Redeemer is not insanity. I obtained Salvation through

Repentance and the New Birth and the sound mind of Christ in me gave me perfect love and cast out all fear. There is absolutely no record anywhere that I ever acted in an obstreperous manner before, during or after my experience at Chattahoochee. I was simply a plain, old-fashioned, outspoken, persistent, Methodist fly in someone's fancy religious ointment.

At Chattahoochee, a psychiatric doctor by the name of Dr. Curtis was assigned to my case. He spoke with a very pronounced accent, perhaps of Russian or Germanic origin and he wore real heavy and thick glasses. I think that from the beginning, he likely had plans to experiment with me. Looking back on my ordeal, I feel that what he needed were spiritual treatments that only Jesus can give. At times he would confront patients and openly explode with an intense rage. One day, as I was walking down the hall, I happened to meet Dr. Curtis and we both stopped facing each other. He was taller than I was and as I looked up into his reddened face, he literally went into a rage and with contorted features screamed at me, "*You vassst preee—ching!*" and abruptly continued on his way. It is a given truth that I was speechless at the uniquely reprehensible behavior of this strange man.

On another occasion, I met him in the hallway and since I had heard that Adele was sick and was aware that she and the boys needed me, I got Dr. Curtis to stop and I begged him to allow me to go before the staff of doctors in order to see if I could be released to go home. Dr. Curtis was a nervous man and perhaps he had some type of nervous tick or condition. When I told him that I loved my wife and I wanted to help her, his face turned red and contorted, and then he screamed at me, "*You are ly-ying!*" He gave me no answer about meeting with the staff of doctors or about going home. He just walked away. I have never seen a physician or psychiatrist before or after with such manifestly strange behavior. The rhetoric and pejorative attitude of this doctor personally directed towards me was as gnarly as the cypress trees in the Florida swamps. A number of others and I are convinced that Dr. Curtis's revealing statement, "*You vassst preeee-ching!*" confirmed the real and only reason I was arrested, incarcerated and committed to an insane asylum. He was the one official authority that would have known exactly why I was in Chattahoochee and he verbalized the precise reason. No element of doubt exists.

I really don't have words adequate to describe the horror, apprehension and stress of being involuntarily confined in a mental institution especially when the Lord gave me a sound mind based upon my behavior and according to the Word of God. After all is said and done, I strongly believe that much of what is termed insanity is really the work of demons and Jesus Christ gave His disciples the authority to cast out any evil spirits. (Matthew 10:1) Cut off from family, friends and the open fellowship of fellow Christians, I hungered and thirsted after Righteousness and the filial fellowship of the called out assembly. No regular church services were available for me to attend and the spiritual time of Church fellowship (Ecclesia) was what I missed the most. The old-fashioned, joyous, Holy Spirit directed, "Shouting Methodist" style of meetings was exactly the catalyst that sparked the conflict in carnal minds that found the Old Time Religion repugnant. Some warmth of emotion in religion is good, even the Lord Jesus wept and the Apostles worshipped the Lord in Spirit and in Truth.

I found the best form of Church deprivation therapy was to sing spiritual hymns at every opportunity. I count it an honor if the part cast in the 1990; film "Chattahoochee" portrayed me as the hymn-singing inmate except that the real Chattahoochee was an earthly hell, not a glamorized, commercialized Hollywood movie. Ironically, one of the most popular hymns that we sang during this time was: "The Love of God", written in 1917, by Frederick M. Lehman (1868-1953). This song was based on the Jewish poem- Haddamut, written in 1050 in the Aramaic language by a Jewish Cantor named Meir Ben Isaac Nehorai in Worms, Germany. The third stanza had been found written in pencil on the wall of a deceased patient's room in an insane asylum. I feel that the author of this beautiful verse was very likely a sane person and possibly the victim of religious persecution. The Medieval "Holy" Inquisition was famous for its torture and murder of Christians and Jews and used asylums as part of its heinous program.

The perpetrators of my involuntary confinement in Chattahoochee undoubtedly intended that I fade away in an asylum but it appears that the Almighty had other plans for my life and limited my stay to just over three months. The comforting verses found in Romans 8:35 and 39 remind us: "Who shall separate us from the Love of Christ? Nothing and no one shall be able to separate us from the love of God, which is in Christ Jesus our Lord". Truly, nothing on earth can separate us from the pure love of God. The spiritual odyssey of Chattahoochee was living proof of the veracity of Scripture, for me as well as for others.

In 1958, Chattahoochee was known for its infamous "Back Yards." These were special wards in an older building where patients categorized as terminal cases were sent. Generally, a patient sent to the "Back Yards" would only leave the institution in a casket and many of the dead didn't get very far. The swamp and woods behind the state hospital contains a great cemetery of discarded, forgotten and thrown away humanity. We were always under the threat of being sent to the "Back Yards." Almost every day, two orderlies would come to the front wards with the familiar suit of clothing, which consisted of a pair of tough denim overalls, a pair of leather brogans and a straight jacket. Some unfortunate person would be taken away to that terminal place of abode. We never knew when they would be coming for one of us. There were many sleepless nights when I would lay awake in my bed shivering with dread and fearful that this would be my fate.

The staff of doctors had the authority and the means to administer a wide range of drugs, shock therapy and also frontal lobotomies. A frontal lobotomy was a relatively quick and simple surgical procedure whereby the front lobe of the human brain would be permanently severed. Many times after this procedure is done, a person can become a vegetable until death loosens all earthly bonds. Many electric shock treatments were administered to inmates as well as insulin shots. Thank God, I was never given any of these treatments. I strongly believe that it was the miraculous hand of God that protected me from physical and mental destruction performed in the 1950's in the name of progressive, modern, "science," psychiatry, and medicine.

The barbaric angels of pseudo-science even destroyed the mind of a Nobel Prize winning writer and author. Ernest Hemingway's photographic memory and great literary ability was effectively fried by the means of electric shock treatments or ECT. Mr. Hemingway said: *"Well, what is the sense of ruining my head and erasing my memory, which is my capital, and putting me out of business? It was a brilliant cure but we lost the patient"*. In 1961, just days after he was released from the facility where he had been involuntarily subjected to prolonged ECT, Ernest Hemingway committed suicide. The use of ECT provides no legitimate cure for any form of mental illness and the damage is usually permanent. Profit conscious doctors misusing electricity to barbarically abuse people should apply regular ECT "treatments" on themselves and on their colleagues as a form of "therapy" to "cure" their own psychological problems. Frying the intellect and memory of human beings with ECT is no more an effective cure for any illness than a lead pipe forcefully applied to the victim's skull. God has a much better way to treat the disturbed among us with- Love, empathy and family networks, prayer and counseling, support groups and environmental therapy, and the casting out of demons when necessary followed by the calming effect of practical, Biblical, problem-solving remedies for mind, body and soul.

All throughout the three months I was in Chattahoochee, the doctors thought that I was taking the 400 daily milligrams of Thorazine but they never discovered that the toilets were swallowing the institutions' drugs instead. My diagnosis was positive without the all-supreme scientific "help" of any mind numbing drugs, insulin, shock therapy or lobotomies. Some of the inmates at Chattahoochee would smoke cigarettes almost indiscriminately throughout the wards creating great discomfort to patients allergic to the smoke. Other inmates would chew their tobacco and drool onto their pajamas leaving distinct and smelly stains. Some aspects of the institution were truly disgusting, adding a surreal quality.

I discovered and met two other Christians at Chattahoochee who were put there for their Christian testimony, nothing more, and nothing less. One man was from Tampa and another man, Phillip Leslie Cooper, was from Orlando. This dear Brother in Christ had been a member of the Church of the Nazarene and had been baptized in the Spirit of the Lord Jesus Christ and was on fire to evangelize.

His family had apparently been shocked by the dramatic change in his behavior and had him consigned to Chattahoochee much the same way my family had done. After we made our acquaintance, the three of us began to have Bible readings and prayer in our rooms. It wasn't long before the doctors found out about the Christian fellowship and broke it up. They began locking our rooms during the day. We weren't even allowed to have prayer together. There was another patient that attended our prayer meetings and gave his heart to Christ. A few days later, he was transferred to the "Back Yards" and some time later on, I saw him looking out a window. After that, I never saw him again. At the very rear of the "Back Yard" ward was a large back porch. I walked back there several times and I observed several patients rocking themselves in rocking chairs for hours at a time. I believe some of them had undergone brain surgery.

Pastor David Ebersole, Brother Lloyd Clymer, and some other Mennonites came to visit with me and talked with the doctors on my behalf and they told the doctors that I didn't belong in the state hospital. After a while I became so hungry to be able to go to church and to preach the Gospel of Jesus Christ but all I could do was to do a very limited amount of witnessing on the ward. We were allowed to read our own Bible individually but not together in a group. We couldn't have a group prayer meeting of any kind nor could we openly tell anyone about Jesus Christ. Witnessing was strictly limited to when no staff was around. I believe God sent me as a Missionary to Chattahoochee and Brother Cooper and I saw at least one convert exercise real faith in Jesus Christ which made it worth being there. God was much greater than the state hospital.

Phillip Cooper was a fine young Christian man and being very zealous for Christ, he would witness when others were around. His doctor found out about his persistence, called him in and told him that this had to stop and that if he persisted in his behavior, his Thorazine would be doubled. Well, that is what happened. I admired his loyalty and zeal but I believe tact would have been the better part of wisdom. They increased his Thorazine to 800 milligrams a day and from then on, Brother Phillip Cooper was almost unable to even walk. He spent most of his time lying down and immobile, barely functional. I begged him not to swallow the drug but to no avail. When I finally left Chattahoochee, he was still just dragging along in a stupor. I never knew what happened to him until a visit to Chattahoochee accompanied by my son Silas and Brother Rodney Wisham in the summer of 2003. Brother Phillip Leslie Cooper also survived Chattahoochee.

Social dances were held for the patients down at the gymnasium but no church services. One Sunday morning, a man came and played an organ at the gym and he played a few church hymns. I would sing my heart out and cry. This was the first time in my life since I had become a Christian that in spite of my desire to attend church, I was not able to do so. There was nothing I could do about it. My freedom, my citizenship, my pursuit of spiritual happiness and all my civil rights had been completely taken away. I had been reduced from a free American citizen to a man without a country and a prisoner of hope. *"Turn ye to the stronghold, ye prisoners of hope."* (Zecariah 9:12) I was relieved of my driver's license, deprived of my liberty, I couldn't vote or buy and sell real estate, and I was subject to the mercy or lack thereof by one or more so-called doctors who held me in little esteem.

Also on our ward, they had several types of therapy including music. About once a week, a lady would come in and play the piano. Her repertoire included some little choruses and worldly tunes. One day, I asked the orderly if they had any church hymnals and he brought some out and I asked the pianist to play some of these hymns. Well, for a whole hour or more, several other inmates and I kept this lady playing nothing but old-fashioned Gospel music as we sang, and sang praises unto God. I really got a blessing in my soul and I don't know what others got out of the experience but I was having church. The Bible says in Psalm 22:3 that God inhabits the praises of His people. This simply means that God made a way for some of us held in Chattahoochee to be elevated into God's presence and power through singing praises and worshipping the God of the Prophets, Apostles and the Redeemed of all ages.

The Lord blessed me in many ways. After I was given outside privileges and could walk around on the hospital grounds, I would walk down the hill toward the sewage disposal plant near a wooded area. It entered my mind several times to effect an escape but I sensed a still small voice saying, "*Son, just be patient, I am working this out in my own good time, then you will be glad that I did it my way*". That is exactly what I did in obedience to God's leading. I had a perfect record at Chattahoochee and kept it that way as long as I was there. We also had leather working therapy where we learned to tool leather goods. I made several items including a nice hand-tooled leather handbag for my wife that we still have and treasure. Many nights I lay awake wondering what would happen to me. I would also pray for hours at a time. I prayed for Adele and all of my family and for everyone that I could remember.

After my second month at Chattahoochee, one day I had a pleasant surprise. My wife and sons James and Silas, my Dad, along with an older brother and his wife came to see me. The doctors allowed me to go with my family downtown to have dinner in a restaurant. I could hardly believe they were there. It was very good to see my family again, especially my wife and boys. After dinner, we went back to the hospital grounds and sat out under some trees and talked for a while. It was nearing the middle of the afternoon and I noticed that no one had mentioned anything about me being released or going home. I spoke up and asked them if they were going to talk to the doctors about my going home. No one said anything until finally, my sister-in-law snapped back with sharp, precise words. She said, "*Jack! We are not taking you home, you are going to stay here and get some more treatments and get well!*" With that retort, the visit ended and they all got into the car and left me there. We were being observed from inside since almost immediately, two well-built order-lies all dressed in white came walking up to me and without a word, one on each side, led me, not to an angelic encounter but to a locked ward to start all over again. All my privileges were taken away and I have never experienced such despair. It was very hard for me for the next few weeks and by the Grace of God, on August 26, 1958, I was finally discharged from the Florida State Hospital at Chattahoochee. My worst experience with social ostracism was ended.

FOURTEEN

Veteran's Administration Hospital at Gulf Port, MS

From Tuesday, May 20, 1958, until Monday, August 25, 1958, there are no further entries in my personal diary. In Chattahoochee, writing things down was a very suspicious activity. Democratic notions such as freedom of speech and of the press were out of the question in such a tightly monitored environment. Even Kenneth Donaldson had some trouble in Chattahoochee writing his diary and manuscript for his book: "Insanity Inside Out".

It turns out that my youngest brother had spoken with our Florida Congressman and on my behalf negotiations had been made to transfer me to the Veteran's Administration Hospital at Gulf Port, Mississippi. It helped to be an honorably discharged military veteran. A post-Chattahoochee entry from my personal diary for 1958 reveals:

Tuesday, August 26, 1958. "Was discharged from Chattahoochee and taken to the Veteran's Administration Hospital facility in Gulf Port, Mississippi."

I was taken by one or two staff members from Chattahoochee to the Veteran's Administration Hospital in Gulf Port. It took about a half a day to get there by automobile. I must say that the grounds were absolutely beautiful. We were right along the beachfront of the Gulf of Mexico. As usual, I was placed on a locked ward for observation for two weeks and I was assigned to a psychiatrist. The morning after my arrival, I was brought before this particular doctor and it was altogether different at Gulf Port than at Chattahoochee. The doctor was very pleasant and after looking over my records, he just plainly said, "You don't belong here, you should have been discharged at the Florida State Hospital." I replied, "Yes sir, I know that."

Wednesday the 27th. "At Gulf Port, Mississippi. The doctor told me that I didn't belong there. I knew that."

They never gave me any drugs or medicine in the V. A. Hospital at Gulf Port, not even an aspirin. The hospital facility had a swimming pool that I used quite often to keep up my daily exercise regimen and stay in physical shape. While there, I would also take long brisk hikes along the beach. After a few weeks, they wrote my wife a letter to come to Gulf Port and discuss our future plans. She never came to visit and didn't even answer their letter. All that the Veteran's Administration needed was for some member of my family to sign me out. I wrote to my sister and brother-in-law in Pensacola to come and visit me but it was a full month before they came. At this time, I was assigned to a woman doctor named Denham and when they went in to talk with the doctor, I was sitting outside the door. I overheard my brother-in-law ask Dr. Denham about what kind of treatments I was receiving and she told him that I wasn't being given any. This was a big surprise for my sister and brother-in-law. In reality, I didn't take any medicines or receive any treatments at Chattahoochee. Some family members and doctors had only assumed that I had been mentally unhinged and that I had received some treatments in order to get well.

After months of up close and personal examinations and observation at Chattahoochee and in the Veteran's Hospital at Gulfport, with no medications, treatment or operations, I was very well in Christ Jesus. My overall stay in Gulf Port was very brief. I was admitted on August 26, 1958, and discharged on October 9, 1958.

The total time I was detained at Bronson and at Gulf Port lasted exactly five months, from May 9th to October 9, 1958.

Thursday, October 9, 1958. "I was released from the V. A. Hospital in Gulf Port, Mississippi. My sister and brother-in-law came to see me and when they told the doctor I could live with them in Pensacola, they released me immediately. Thank you Jesus!"

That is all the doctors wanted to hear and within 30 minutes, I was signed out of the Veteran's Administration Hospital and we were on our way to Pensacola. I was praising and thanking God!

At Asbury College in Wilmore, Kentucky- September 1950
Left to Right- unknown, unknown, unknown and Jack Griffin.

The evangelistic team of Jack Griffin and
Brother Barney Young in 1952, with the tent at Dowling Park, FL

Baptist Purity Church- Pastor Luther Turner and family
in 1952, near Salem, Florida.

Jack and Paul Griffin with some of the children
at the Verbenadale Church near Williston, Florida, 1953

Jack Griffin picking cotton near Hopeful, Georgia
in the summer of 1954, with members of the Wisham family

Jack Griffin with the Faith Gospel Mission tent in 1954,
in the front yard of Mr. Edgar Wisham near Vada, Georgia.

Portrait of the Jack and Adele Griffin family
At Chiefland, Florida, 1955 — 1956

Paul and Jack with the 1950, Chevrolet truck and Gospel signs

My tourist visa card to enter Cuba, February 20, 1958

Jack with Pastor Urra's son in front of The Open Bible Church
in the town of Guanajay near Havana, Cuba, 1958

Brother John Kaufman with Pastor Urra and family
at the Open Bible Church, Guanajay, Cuba 1958

INQUISITION OF INCOMPETENCY
(CHAPTER 394 FLORIDA STATUTES)

STATE FORM XL-10

In the Court of the County Judge,

in and for _____Levy_____ County,
State of Florida.

Jack Ray Griffin   }   Inquisition of Incompetency

Order for Delivery of Mentally Incompetent to State Hospital
In the Name of the State of Florida, to the Sheriff of said County:

WHEREAS, on the __9th__ day of _____May_____, 19__58__, this court upon petition presented thereto did issue an order directing the sheriff of said county to summon forthwith the committee heretofore appointed to inquire into the competency of one __Jack Ray Griffin__ _____, a resident of the county aforesaid, and

WHEREAS, said committee has made its report to this court to the effect that its members find the said _____Jack Ray Griffin_____ to be mentally incompetent by reason of:

_____Schizophrenia_____

and to require confinement or restraint to prevent self-injury or violence to others, and the court having taken other evidence on said petition and the said__Jack Ray Griffin__has by this court been adjudged mentally incompetent within the meaning of the statute in such cases made and provided.

It further appearing from the evidence taken by the court that the physical condition of the said incompetent __Jack Ray Griffin_____, is such that _____can safely make the trip to the Florida State Hospital without endangering h__is__ life or health.

You are therefore, commanded forthwith to deliver the said incompetent_____ Jack Ray Griffin _____to the Superintendent of the Florida State Hospital for care, maintenance and treatment, as provided by law, together with a transcript of all proceedings in this case.

DONE AND ORDERED in_____Bronson_____, Florida,
_____May 12,_____ 19__58__

s/ W. F. Anderson (seal)
County Judge

Document- Inquisition of Incompetency, May 9, 1958

INQUISITION OF INCOMPETENCY
(CHAPTER 994 FLORIDA STATUTES AS AMENDED)

STATE FORM XL-7 REV.

In the Court of the County Judge,

in and for _____ **LEVY** _____ County,

State of Florida.

JACK RAY GRIFFIN

Inquisition of Incompetency

Report of Committee Finding Incompetency

To the Judge of said Court:

Your committee appointed to examine into the alleged incompetency of _____

Jack Ray Griffin _____ , *having made a thorough examination of the mental and physical*

condition of the said alleged incompetent, begs to submit the following report: 1. *We determine that*

he is incompetent, the apparent cause being _____ Schizophrenia _____

2. *The same is acute* _____ ; *chronic* _____ X

3. *The particular hallucinations are* _____ some paranoia _____ ;

h is *propensities are* _____ fight _____

4. *H* is *age is* _____ 43 _____ . 5. *he does* _____ not _____ *require*

mechanical restraint to prevent h im *from self-injury or violence to others.* 6. *He* _____

_____ *is* _____ *destitute and is* _____ *eligible to be committed as such.*

7. *Said person or the estate of said person is* not *sufficient to support and maintain said person*

in full or in part, if _____ *he is committed to the Director of Mental Health for assignment to such*

State Hospital as the Director may designate. 8. *Said Person does* not *have relatives who are*

legally responsible for his *support and maintenance and who are* _____ *able to pay in full or in*

part for the treatment of said person in a Florida State Hospital; the names and addresses of said

relatives are as follows:

_____ *Address* _____

_____ *Address* _____

Respectfully submitted this _____ 12th _____ *day of* _____ **May** _____ , 19 58 .

_____ , M.D.

_____ , M.D.

Willie L. Green

Committee

Document- Report of Committee, May 12, 1958

138

ADMISSION

Mr. Jack Ray Griffin, A-27770 ⟨ *⟩   Levy

NAME   COUNTY

5-19-58   43   158   5'10"   White

ADMISSION DATE   AGE WT. HT.   RACE

Male   Blue   Sandy   Ruddy

SEX   EYES   HAIR   COMPLEXION

                  Married   Not stated

OTHER MARKS   CIVIL CONDITION   RELIGION

Rt. 1 Box 46 - Chiefland, Fla.

HOME ADDRESS   OCCUPATION

Mrs. Anna A. Griffin - Rt. 1 Box 46 - Chiefland, Fla.

NAME AND ADDRESS

Wife   Person left before signing papers   C. Edwards, Att.

RELATIONSHIP   BROUGHT BY   ADMITTED BY

8-26-58

DISCHARGED WT.   DIED   FURLOUGHED WT.

ESCAPED Archives Acc. # 74128 - SRC # 9185 - cts. # 391 RETURNED

(OVER)

Document- Admission to Chattahoochee, May 19, 1958

A pencil drawing of a psychiatric evaluation and verdict-
"You Vasssst Preeee-ching!"

Adele's Christian baptism in Oklahoma, November 1958.

In Court of County Judge
Levy County
State of Florida

JACK R. GRIFFIN } INQUISITION OF INCOMPETENCY

ORDER RESTORING JUDICIAL SANITY

This matter coming on this day to be heard upon the petition filed in this court for the purpose of having the sanity and competency of ____ **Jack R. Griffin** ____ judicially determined and no objections having been filed in this court to said petition, from the evidence introduced at the hearing on said petition, the court finds and decrees:

1. That the said ____ **Jack R. Griffin** ____ is of sound mind judicially and is capable of managing **his** own affairs.

2. That the said ____ **Jack R. Griffin** ____ be immediately restored to **his** personal liberty.

3. That the (guardian) (committee) (trustee) of said ____ shall within ____ days from this date make full settlement with said ____ , so restore to the status of judicial sanity, of all h___ property in (their) ch___ custody and control, under penalty of contempt of this court and the punishment thereof.

DONE AND ORDERED in ____ Bronson ____ Florida, ____ January 22, ____ 1960

signature
County Judge

Filed and recorded January
22, 1960, In competency Record
#1, page 122 .

W. F. Anderson, County Judge
By: *signature*
Clerk

Document- Restoration of Judicial Sanity, January 22, 1960

Faith Gospel Mission to the Navajo Nation,
Photo of Jack and Adele taken at Hogback Mountain, January 1960

On the mountain road, state of Tamaulipas, Mexico in 1961
Brother Lopez with our 1960 Opel and 1951 Ford 1-ton truck

Our missionary camp on the bank of the Chihui River, 1961.

Faith Gospel Mission team fording the Chihui River in 1961

Pastor- Jose Ernesto Lopez singing and preaching to attentive audience in the mountain village of Rancho Nuevo, 1961

Brother Lopez and a group of people in a mountain village, 1961

Sister- Gloria Gracia interpreting a message from the Word of God into Spanish with Jack and Adele Griffin, 1961-1962

Silas, Paul & Mexican boys hauling a water barrel on a wagon, 1962

Interpreter-Dora Silva and Pastor Jose Lopez conducting
an evangelistic street meeting in a mountain village
in the state of Coahuila, NE Mexico in 1968

Jack and John Griffin, Pastor- Jose Lopez, Rodney and Patrice
Wisham, with Pastor and Mrs. Harrell ca. 1975, at Bainbridge.
(Used by permission of The Post-Searchlight, Bainbridge, GA)

Brother Pablo Aguirre, Jack and Pastor Lopez with adobes, 1970

Brother Rodney Wisham, Adele and Jack Griffin with
Pastor- Jose Lopez at Ejido Alto de Norias, Coahuila, 1973

Missionary- Rodney Wisham, Pastor- Jose Ernesto Lopez,
and Pastor- Pablo Aguirre building the mission Church
at Ejido El Pelial, in the state of Coahuila, 1975

Pastor – Pablo Aguirre preaching the Word of God
in the Faith Gospel Mission Church at La Tortuga, Coahuila, 1977

Waiting for the train to arrive at Estacion Fraustro, Coahuila
in 1978. Silas Griffin, Bro. Lopez's daughters, Patricia and
Rodney Wisham with children and Brother Daniel Aguirre

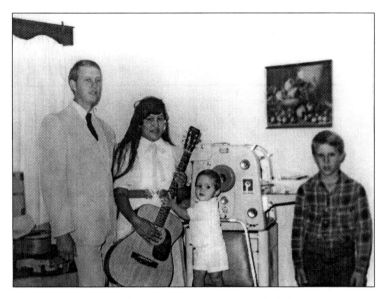

Silas, Abigail, Ivy, and Aaron Griffin at
The Evangelical Church in Aconchi, Sonora- Mexico, 1986

Abigail Griffin with her sister- Priscilla Calderon
leading children in Gospel choruses in the home of
the Barrios family at Sinoquipe, Sonora- Mexico, 1986

Pastor- Israel Guevara with missionaries- John Cantral and Silas Griffin in the Sonora River Valley, central Sonora- 1987

Evangelist- Jack Griffin and Mexican friends at the grave of Pastor- Jose E. Lopez near the train station at Ejido Fraustro, 2004

FIFTEEN

Thank God, We are Free!

"The Lord looseth the prisoners." **(Psalm 146:7)**

I venture to say, based upon my personal experience that around the United States, there have been many Christians summarily and unceremoniously dumped like some waste product into mental hospitals. Many of these servants of God could have left those places had there been some one in their family to sign them out or had the staff complied with the laws. These are the unloved, unwanted, unclaimed and forgotten Americans and it happens in many other places in the world.

At the point in time when I received my new life as the gift of God, I felt like a free bird from prison flown and after my release from the oppression of Chattahoochee, I felt the Divine Blessing of freedom all over again. After three months at Chattahoochee and two months in Gulf Port, I was, thank God, free at last! My faith in God and the deep-rooted resolve to serve Him was now much more firm being built on the only solid foundation, Christ the Rock of my Salvation. My faith in God was tried and tested in the fire of persecution and in spite of my human frailty, my human fear of the unknown and the uncertainty of a clouded future, I can truthfully declare before God and the world that my faith in God never wavered. I trusted in God for salvation and deliverance from evil and He never failed me and He never will fail His people. I would have never dreamt of this happening to myself or to any one, especially to Christians in These United States of America. This personal experience serves to show that Satan has the power to completely deceive religious people, to maliciously persecute God's people and to play his part in effecting God's sovereign plan of the ages. God's divine purpose is fulfilled in one's life in spite of the heathen raging and the world's rejection of Christ.

Denominations such as the Mennonites, and other religious individuals such as Ghandi, aren't the only ones in the world to practice the most effective protest possible against discrimination, invective, and persecution. It appears that the form of protest that I used in dealing with incarceration without Actus Rea and Mens Rea and the subsequent deprivation of my civil, human and spiritual rights by the authorities in Florida, was the form of protest that Jesus manifested in His way of dealing with the overwhelming injustice of sinful humanity. The Prophet Jeremiah said that "*justice is where God sits*", and the Prophet Micah said, "*Justice is the place where God lives*". A life is transformed by justice and God's justice provides for the type of freedom wherein no one can keep the pure in heart in chains of darkness.

Non-violent protest against injustice is the most effective method of dealing with the evil motivation and power behind injustice. This form of protest by a Born-Again, Holy Spirit filled Christian oftentimes destroys the will of the enemies of God. I was not a person given to violent habits and when arrested, charged and incarcerated, my protest was more powerful than the weapons formed against me. After less than six months, there were no weapons left to be thrown against me. There was no legitimate case against God's servant and I had to be set free. All that begins in God's peaceful manner ends well. "*And we know that all things work together for good to them that love God, to them who are the called according to his purpose.*" (Romans 8:28)

Jesus Christ was the supreme model of non-violent protest. No human act or endeavor can ever surpass the universal impact of the arrest, trial, crucifixion, death, burial and glorious resurrection of our Lord. Jesus volitionally laid down his life and took up the glorified life to give Believers eternal life. In the course of human endeavors, non-violent protest may or may not achieve the complete removal of colonialism, injustice, segregation, or political tyranny. The central fact is very clear and indisputably true- Jesus Christ took away the sins of the whole world and in the process of providing Salvation to all who believe, the violence was done to Him, NOT by Him. *"Like a sheep He was led to the slaughter..."* (Acts 8:32)

In stark contrast, the Biblical record in Acts 9:1 says: *"Saul, yet breathing out threatenings and slaughter against the disciples of the Lord, went unto the high priest."* This verse very clearly gives us the full picture of the world's condition and its reaction to God's grace, love, and truth manifested in the lives of the Believers. Such obedient Believers who are truly filled with God's Spirit are over-comers and may be beaten down and locked up, persecuted and martyred but ultimately they are not overcome by evil. In Genesis chapters 2 and 3, the fall of Eve and Adam into the sin of disobedience is in direct relation to their unbelief in God's plain directive concerning not eating of the tree of knowledge of good and evil. In Genesis chapter 4, the first murder was committed based on Cain's unbelief in God's directive concerning an acceptable sacrifice of atonement. The greatest evil in the world is plainly, the sin of UNBELIEF. The following scriptures confirm this truth. Psalm 78:32, Eccl. 9:3, Is. 53:1, Matthew 13:58, Luke 24:11, John 8:24, 12:44-48, 16:8 & 9, Romans 1:28 & 29, 2 Corin. 4:4, Hebrews 3:12, Jude 5, and Rev. 21:8. Some people and organizations differ greatly with inerrant Biblical truth when they state that one issue or another on their activist agenda is the greatest evil in the world. *"He that believeth on the Son hath everlasting life: and he that believeth not the Son shall not see life; but the wrath of God abideth on him."* (John 3:36) The Word of God declares that unbelief and disobedience will keep a soul from entering into Heaven. *"He that believeth on him is not condemned: but he that believeth not is condemned already, because he hath not believed in the name of the only begotten Son of God."* (John 3:18) Jesus is therefore the one and only global Savior. This is the basis for worldwide Christian missions. God has ordained that everybody ought to know who Jesus is. Herein is the love of God manifested. Let all creatures, regardless of size, status and distance, acknowledge and worship the Lord and Savior- Jesus Christ of Nazareth.

On the matter of being faithful to Christ under the extreme duress of religious persecution, Born-Again, Holy Spirit filled Christians can't go under for going over! Amen! On the matter of a question of standards, society must have an established set of ethical, judicial, legal, moral, social, and spiritual standards in order to function for any length of time. Far too often, the line of distinction between good and evil becomes blurred and distorted through human care-lessness and the secular processes of humanistic and socialistic redefinition and revisionism. It is precisely at this point when the application of the Divine code of standards for moral and spiritual conduct becomes all the more urgent for humanity and relevant for the individual. God's code of moral and spiritual standards is not wrapped up in some obtuse form of existentialism nor secreted away in some notion such as the "DaVinci code", or hidden like some "Holy Grail." God's moral and spiritual code is the Holy Bible. I would add that when applying the permanent principles of the Bible, Blackstone, and the Constitution, we can't go wrong.

The Gospel message that God delivered to me to declare to the world is based upon the bedrock of the Holy Bible, not the fickle traditions of men. The most relevant and pressing Biblical question for the human race today is: "What will you do with Jesus Christ, accept and obey Him or reject Him"? Today's corrupt and sinful world demands a clear-cut, unambiguous, positive declaration of moral and spiritual guidance from God. Biblical Christianity is the salt that preserves a society that is acceptable to humanity and Divinity. The very same spiritual drive that urged John Wesley to repent of his sins and to trust implicitly in Christ alone for salvation and to seek the fullness of the Holy Spirit in order to tolerate the belittling and violent mobs, to preach from his father's grave, to travel from continent to continent, to continuously exhort all men everywhere to repent and believe the Gospel, is the very same drive that has compelled millions of believers across the broad stretch of world history to preach Christ and Him crucified, risen and glorified— at any cost. It is the same spiritual drive that compelled thousands of circuit riding "saddlebag" preachers such as Robert S. Sheffey in

Virginia to leave the material comforts of home and travel through the wilderness and mountainous regions searching for the lost sheep and to bring them safely into the fold of the Great Shepherd.

The compelling call of the Holy Spirit made Godly missionaries out of other men such as David Brainerd, David Livingston, Henry Martyn and Samuel Morris. The same drive compelled Thomas Griffin to consecrate his life upon God's altar as a youth in Georgia and to spend his years on earth in the faithful service of the King of Glory. It is the same drive that compelled me to render unto God that which is God's for His Glory and Honor and for the salvation of souls into God's Heavenly Kingdom. This is a reasonable service of ministry evidenced in Scripture and in the lives of God's people.

I fully concur with the compelling statement made by John Wesley: "We therefore not only allow, but earnestly exhort all who seek after true religion to use all the reason which God hath given them in seeking out the things of God". (From Jackson's Edition of John Wesley's Journal- Public Domain) (Cragg- http://www.gbgm-umc.org/sonorafirst/windex.html This very same goal has been my consistent conviction and practice throughout the years.

At the time of my release, the doctors at the V. A. Hospital in Gulf Port advised me not to go back to my wife since it was very likely that she would cause me further trouble. After two weeks staying with my sister and brother-in-law at Pensacola, I couldn't stand it any longer. I had to go to Chiefland and see about Adele and the boys. When I arrived at home, Adele greeted me with the question, "How did you get out"? I just told her, "They opened the door and I walked out free". I could tell that Adele wasn't very well and that she was a very sick woman. She was taking six kinds of medicine. I immediately took her to the hospital in Live Oak and they admitted her and started running some lab tests on her. We lived about fifty miles away from the hospital and I had to take care of the boys and commute back and forth while she was there. Unbeknown to me, some preacher who visited the sick in the hospital, came to talk with Adele three times and she related to me that after the preacher's third visit, she went into the bathroom and kneeled to pray and that God had saved her.

When I came back to the hospital on my next visit a day or two later, I noticed that something had apparently happened to Adele. She had a radiant look on her face and when I walked over to her bed, she asked me to pray for her. I knelt by her bed and prayed as humbly as I knew how for God to heal Adele. She had not told me that God had saved her. God instantly healed her and the pain left her side. Adele was free at last and she too had a new life and a new bill of health. The doctors ran some more tests and could find nothing wrong with her. Her condition had completely changed.

This was a real miracle of God and Adele testified that she was now saved and healed by the power of God. Adele asked me to forgive her for sending me to Chattahoochee and she also voluntarily confessed her wrongdoing in other secret sins committed while I was overseas. She was released from the hospital two days later and I took her home and we discovered upon arrival that Silas was sick with a high fever. We both knelt by his bedside and prayed and asked God to touch him and Silas was healed and before long, went outside to play. God still saves, heals and delivers today. God is not dead, He is still alive and on the Sovereign throne of heaven!

SIXTEEN

Christian Soldiers in Missionary Work

"Do all the good you can, by all the means you can, in all the ways you can, in all the places you can, at all the times you can, to all the people you can, as long as ever you can."
—John Wesley

Things in our home were very different now and for the first time, Adele wanted to go with me to church and to the mission field. She didn't want to wait to sell our house so we rented it out. We packed our clothing and personal things into a small 16-foot camp trailer and left Florida to go to Farmington, New Mexico to begin a mission among the Navajo Indians. The Lord blessed us with all of our needs taken care of. He is still doing the same today. On the way to New Mexico in the fall of 1958, Adele was baptized in a lake as we passed through Oklahoma and the Lord blessed us with a larger travel trailer that we paid for in cash. Adele and I have made it a practice all these years to never buy anything unless we can pay cash for it. If we don't have the money to pay in cash, we just don't buy it. We economize and save a lot of money by paying cash and I believe that the world would be in much better economic condition if more people followed this rule. John Wesley set a very good example in the economics area of Christian lifestyle. This type of Christian lifestyle enabled us to move on to our next phase of ministry.

By this time, Adele and I had been married for 23 years. I had been saved for nine years and now Adele had given her heart to the Lord and was a baptized believer. In reality, this was the beginning of our second honeymoon. I believe that it was about the first week of November of 1958, that we left Florida to go to the mission field in the southwest region of the United States. Since that time we have returned to Florida only to visit and not to live. No one in our own families has ever taken a serious interest in our missionary and evangelistic trip to Cuba, among the American Indians or in Old Mexico. I believe that this attitude can be attributed to either a complete lack of understanding of what it means to have a Divine call to work in God's harvest fields or it is indicative of sectarianism based on a denominational and doctrinal bias. There may even be a deep root of bitterness and prejudice toward the American Indians for the deaths of the Griffin twins killed in an ambush at the Bashi Skirmish in Clarke County, Alabama in the war of 1812.

You have to have a special vision or impression from God in order to leave all and go by Faith to where God leads you. The Bible says in Proverbs 29:18: "*Without a vision, the people perish*". And in 2 Samuel 22:20: "*He brought me forth also into a large place*". Brother Larson, a member of the Verbenadale Church near Williston, Florida, had told us about the Navajo Indian People in the South West. I felt that God had used Brother Larson's influence to give us some direction as to where to go. It has been a great joy for me to be out in the great work of God and see how God supplies all of our needs, "pressed down, and shaken together and running over", to the extent that we have many times shared with others. When we arrived in Farmington, NM, we parked our trailer in Pruitt's Trailer Park and began making contacts with the Navajo Indian tribe. We never could learn the language so we had to find an interpreter. I would always find construction work to supplement our income. We had some Christian friends who would send us some love offerings for the work and this helped a lot. It encouraged us a great deal to know that some one else was interested in our efforts and especially that they were praying for us and the work of the Lord among the American Indian people.

We continued making trips out onto the Navajo Reservation, visiting in their one-room adobe and log houses called Hogan's. We distributed clothing, foodstuffs, Gospel literature, and Bibles among the Navajo. At that time, the Navajo tribe was the largest Indian nation in North America. We loved the Indian people and we have found throughout American history that in general, the Indian has been nobler than the white man. It is a shame the way the whites have treated the Indian people, taking their land, killing off the buffalo and other wild game for sport or to effect genocide, and even attacking their women and children. The Indian people were lied to many times and treated like coyotes or some other wild animal. This type of treatment has never been the will of God and never will be. We continued working among the Navajo during the winter of 1958, throughout 1959, until early 1960. At one point in time, a Mormon family at Hogback Mountain allowed us to use one end of their old trading post for a church. I installed windows and a door, built some benches, and painted a sign that read: *"Faith Gospel Mission to the Navajo"*.

We began having regular evangelistic services in this impromptu church building and attendance started increasing. We were well liked by the Navajo people and our boys played well with the Navajo children. The Mormon family could hear what I was preaching since they had an active trading post on the other end of the same building. One of the reasons that this family allowed us to set up a church here was that they wanted us to counter influence the effects of a nearby liquor store just off the reservation boundary. Some of the Navajo Indian people were heavy drinkers and a significant number of the local Navajo would buy their liquor at this store about a quarter of a mile away from where we were living and ministering. The drunks would continually stagger off from the store and lie passed out on the ground and in the fields around the area.

In January of 1960, during the time that we lived at Waterflow, New Mexico, I received a copy of the Order Restoring Judicial Sanity from Levy County Judge- W. F. Anderson. It states: *"This matter coming on this day to be heard upon the petition filed in this court for the purpose of having the sanity and competency of*

Jack R. Griffin judicially determined and no objections having been filed in this court to said petition, from the evidence introduced at the hearing on said petition, the court finds and decrees: 1.-That the said Jack R. Griffin is of sound mind judicially and is capable of managing his own affairs. 2.-That the said Jack R. Griffin be immediately restored to his personal liberty. Done and ordered in Bronson, Florida, January 22, 1960". (Filed and recorded Jan. 22, 1960, In Competency record # 1, page 122, W. F. Anderson, County Judge, by: Willie L. Green- Clerk) Since then, I have written documentation proving that I am a sane and competent person, that I am able to manage my own business, and that I am a free American citizen. In my new life, I am in the pursuit of God's happiness and neither criminal thought nor deed is committed.

In time, the Mormon family didn't like my Evangelical preaching and before long, ordered us to vacate their property. At first, we didn't know exactly where to move to but God opened a door for us to go out to California and visit an old friend, Brother McNabb who was pastoring a church in the San Joaquin Valley. Brother McNabb and I had entered into a prayer covenant at Suwannee Gardens in 1952, on behalf of the conversion of Adele. God had answered our prayers and Brother McNabb was a special Christian Brother to me. It didn't take us long to be headed out on the highway for California. We crossed the famous Mojave Desert in the summer of 1960, and it was terribly hot. I was getting used to pulling our 40-foot travel trailer by the time we arrived at Pastor McNabb's place in Tulare, California. We tried to find some Indians to minister to up in the mountains but we didn't find many Indians left in that area. I knew that as we traveled westward, we were not really where God wanted us to be. I was not very happy to stumble around like this. We did try to witness for Christ in all the places we went but after a couple of months in California, in the late summer of 1960, we left headed east for Albuquerque, New Mexico.

We had heard of the All Tribes Indian Mission at San Bernalillo near Albuquerque. We stopped there and endeavored to help in this mission work among the Navajo. We started making many trips out onto the reservation with Brother Walker. I bought our son Jimmy a horse and saddle and he enjoyed that very much along with his

Navajo friends. The name of the reservation where we focused our ministry with Brother Walker was Canoncito. It was a part of the larger Navajo reservation containing about 100,000 acres of land. It was in our hearts to continue traveling on to Greenville, Mississippi in order to visit my Aunt Eutie Keel Rivers, my mother's sister. After a couple months of working with All Tribes Mission at Canoncito, we left and headed for Greenville.

We spent the rest of 1960, including the entire winter, living near Greenville. We attended services at a Pentecostal Assembly of God Church in Greenville and one night, we heard another missionary speak who had been down in Old Mexico. He told of the great hunger to hear the Gospel among the Mexican and Indian people. He related how the people would walk for miles and how the women would stand in the hot sun holding their little ones to hear God's message. His mission report of the interest in listening to the Word of God in Mexico fired us up to go to this new field. We strongly felt that this was the most needful of God's fields for us to work in and that this was the place where God wanted us to be.

SEVENTEEN

A Mission by Faith in Mexico, Si Senor!

"Jesus Christ is the same yesterday, today and forever."
Hebrews 13:8

"Jesucristo es el mismo ayer, hoy y por todos los siglos."
Hebreos 13:8

We left Greenville, Mississippi about the last week of January of 1961, and arrived at Brownsville, Texas on the 2nd of February. We parked our travel trailer in a trailer park on the north side of town and within a day or two, we started going across the international border to the city of Matamoros, Tamaulipas. We met some of the local Christians as well as some local Pastors and within a week we were singing some of the Gospel coritos or choruses in Spanish. Gloria A Dios! We started having evangelistic services in people's homes, evangelistic street meetings on both sides of the border, jail services, and visiting in some of the churches.

Within a few weeks after the beginning of 1961, we were going beyond the border zone into some small villages and presently, making trips into the interior to such places as Ciudad Mante and Ciudad Victoria, the capital of the state of Tamaulipas. In the summer of 1961, we pulled our New Moon travel trailer to Ciudad Victoria and rented a trailer spot at a hotel on the edge of the city. This was a temporary headquarters for us and during the month we stayed there, we met the Bailey's who were also missionaries in the area. From Ciudad Victoria, we traveled a narrow and winding dirt road that climbed a large mountain range to a large valley or plateau in a high mountain region. This trip would take at least four hours during the dry season. At times it was so dry we could scoop handfuls of dust that collected under the hood of the truck. The major watershed in this region was dry most of the times we crossed it on our way to the towns and villages in the plateau area. We camped several times near the river ford with our second-hand army tent, pickup truck and camper and 1960, Model Opal Chevrolet. This was an educational adventure for our boys.

I had bought James a horse for $25.00 at Ciudad Victoria and on one occasion he wanted to ride up the mountain road but the horse couldn't make the summit. We loaded the horse into our 1951, Ford, 1-ton stake-body truck and traveled on to the river to make camp. The largest town in the region was the municipal seat of Juamave where we picked up supplies and gasoline before launching out to minister in the remote, rural, mountainous ranches and villages. Gasoline purchases in the remote region involved the transfer of the vital liquid from a 55-gallon drum into a five-gallon can. The gas was then poured from the can into the vehicle tank through a funnel. Many rural people walked, rode on horses and burros and in ox carts. Life was carried on at a much slower pace in Mexico.

We always carried an interpreter on each evangelistic trip. Our ministerial routine was to start at eight in the mornings, visit three or four villages in one day where we preached in the streets and plazas oftentimes to crowds of interested people. We used a battery operated public address system with the same large metal speakers I had taken with me to Cuba to play recorded Gospel music, to announce the meetings and to preach the Word of God to everyone in range. The rural villages we ministered in were: San Antonio, San Juan del Oriente, San Juanita, San Francisco, and San Jose. We intended to construct a church building in Ejido Rancho Nuevo del Sur but this desire never became material.

On several occasions we had evangelistic meetings at the humble home of an elderly woman close to where the dirt road forded the Chihui River and her yard would be filled with country people listening intently to the Word of God. At this time in rural Mexico, the inhabitants of the villages and small towns would flock to the area of the central plaza in the community and stand and listen to the plain preaching of the Gospel. We never used any frivolous techniques or tricks to attract a group of people to preach to. We would get permission from the local government leaders, announce the evangelistic meeting on the public address system and metal speakers, distribute Gospel tracts and witness from house to house, followed by the evangelistic service. The rest was up to God and He never failed us in our endeavors to reach the Mexican people with the message of Salvation.

On one trip to the region, we met another Evangelical Missionary-Sister Marie Searcy. She was a faithful servant of God working for many years in this region. The rough and dusty dirt road that cut across this mountainous region from Ciudad Victoria to Tula is now paved- Highway 101. During the summer of 1961, we met a Pastor-Jose Ernesto Lopez who was with the Church of God in Ciudad Victoria. When he found out that we were missionaries and working by faith, he left his church denomination and started working with us in full-time ministry. As a Missionary team, we made many trips to the villages in the harsh mountain region south of the Ciudad Victoria area. We appreciated his testimony of how he had been born in Buena Vista, Jalisco on November 7, 1935, and as a young man he had been converted from Roman Catholicism to Evangelical Christianity. Brother Lopez had attended the Church of God- Berea Bible School in the City of Obregon, Sonora. After he graduated from Bible school, he was called to pastor several Churches of God and he evangelized in the northeast sector of Mexico in the states of San Luis Potosi, Tamaulipas and Coahuila. Not only did Brother Jose Lopez preach God's Word without fear or favor but also he was a constructor and builder unlike any other national Christian minister we ever met. He endlessly preached out against the doctrinal errors of Romanism, Jehovah's Witnesses and the "Jesus Only" movement. We found that the Missionary's report as given in Mississippi was true and God gave the confirmation for our Ministry in Mexico through the Holy Spirit.

We decided to become established on the border and bought a 2.5 acre parcel of land from Mr. Williams on Gilson Road off Old Highway 77, about three miles north of Brownsville. We parked our 40-foot trailer there and this became our home and mission headquarters for almost ten years. We bought half of the lumber from an old house in town, dismantled the structure and used the solid old lumber to construct a wood frame church building approximately 30 feet by 50 feet. We had a water well drilled, installed a pump and tank, fenced off the acreage for pasture, built a small barn for a milk cow, and fenced an area for chickens. We always had a family garden plot and at least one milk cow.

Shortly after our arrival in Brownsville, we discovered the long-standing popular local tradition of Charro Days. The international border communities of Brownsville and Matamoros conducted a joint, annual, four-day, pre-Lenten festival called Charro Days dating from 1937, when the local Chamber of Commerce organized it. The cities would host parades, street dances, rodeos, mariachi and marimba concerts in the plazas and parks involving participation by the students of both communities. The Immigration and Naturalization Service would allow the Mexican nationals to cross the bridges over the Rio Grande to Brownsville in order to shop locally and participate in the celebrations of Charro Days. We adapted our ministry to the local pace of life on the border and during Charro Days we would host special services known as our annual International Fellowship Meeting at our mission's base. Brethren from the local area as well as from the interior of Mexico would attend the three to four days of evangelistic and fellowship meetings.

Living out on a Missionary field somewhere far away from the place we originate means being separated from friends, family and the routine of what we oftentimes consider civilized society. This separation from family and friends may last for years. I loved my parents very much and I dearly love my brothers and sisters and endeavor to visit them as often as possible. Although communication is open and infrequent, none of my in-laws or family members has come out to visit us on the missionary field except my Uncle

Bunyan Keel and my Aunt Eutie Keel Rivers who did visit with us at Brownsville, Texas. They went with us across the border into Mexico and were so impressed with our church service in a little Mexican farm house that my uncle went around giving each person a piece of money and my aunt went around hugging the women and girls. They wondered why my brothers and sisters didn't help support us in the work and even wrote them about it.

This excerpt from one of our mission newsletters from Brownsville dated November 1963, evidences the nature of the spiritual warfare we were involved in at that time.

"We write this newsletter to let you know that we are still on the firing line for God. We thank each of you for your prayers and the love gifts you have sent us to help in this work of Faith. For about six weeks we have been having street meetings in Brownsville and one Saturday afternoon, a Catholic priest walked right up to us and called one of the workers aside and talked real nasty and said that we were like children and didn't know what we were saying. We have been putting up some Gospel signs that Brother Palmer sent from Virginia. We've had 14 of these signs torn down and we recovered only one. We put two signs on posts in front of the house of Brother Snyder, a blind preacher, in town and someone took the signs, posts and all. We haven't been able to get an interpreter for the past few months so we have been working back and forth across the border giving out tracts, visiting the hospital and having regular services here at the mission. For the past two and one half months, we have had Sister Victoria Zavala and her two-year old baby girl from Pancho Villa, Mexico here with us and she has been a real blessing to us. She is a real Missionary from Mexico. We believe this is God's last call to Mexico and we must not fail to get the true Gospel to them." Your Missionaries to Mexico—Jack, Adele & Boys

On one occasion, I spoke with one of my brother's-in-law who had been promoted to a supervisory position in the Southern Baptist

Church in Florida, about the changes and the drift that occurs over time in denominational bodies and organized religious entities. I told him to drive a stake and as the years go by to assess the amount of doctrinal drift and the lapses and compromises in ethical, moral and spiritual values that oftentimes occur within religions and within the moral, sociological and spiritual parameters of society in general. In other words, I advised him to measure the compromises in beliefs and the shift in values that the Holy Bible identifies as spiritual apostasy even within his own beloved denomination. He became somewhat upset with me over this matter and afterwards, never did accept me as a bonafide Minister of Christ. I believe he would have been equally disturbed with what Rev. Thomas Griffin had to say about the issue. *"If our people are not faithful, God will raise up another sect, for He will have a people."* (Griffin, p. 210)

I still maintain that any religion that names the name of Christ, that shifts its ethical standards, changes its moral values, and lapses in its spiritual beliefs, modifies its Biblical doctrines, and that significantly changes its emphasis on who Jesus Christ really is, has become Apostate. Apostasy is simply a rebellion against the truth and Grace of God. This is precisely what has happened in America and across the world over the last several decades. Some formerly mainstream elements of the Church have drifted away from the Truth of the Gospel founded on the Rock that is the Lord Jesus Christ. These religious elements have shifted to the worldly traditions of men, to false philosophies and doctrines of demons as one Apostle of our Lord put it. Instead of being true Ministers of the Grace of God, they are ravening wolves in sheep's skins. The world has drifted in step with the drifting religious crowd and they are now together so far from shore in a state of spiritual Apostasy that they perniciously declare that the Christians are Right-wing, hard-core conservatives, fundamentalist extremists and damn and decry the True Church for holding the firing line of Truth and Morality for our immutable God. True Christianity is based upon the unchanging, uncompromising, and eternal Word of God, nothing more, and nothing less. Many of the organized major religions of the world and the secular-humanist world in general have shifted so far to the biased, extreme, un-Godly, unbelieving Left that to them, anything from their perspective appears to be extreme and afar off- to the "right". The millions of real born-again, faithful Christians in America and around the world haven't drifted or shifted one whit in belief and doctrine since they are deeply rooted and grounded in the doctrines and truths of the Gospel of Jesus Christ which is allegorically and literally found to be the only bastion of permanence and stability in a corrupted, fickle, and immoral society, world, and universe. The Lord Jesus Christ declared to the world- repent or perish. Hell is forever hot, eternally waterless, filled with hateful demons and is enlarged to accommodate the reprehensible wicked.

One day in n 1963, a little green Volkswagen with Mississippi license plates pulled up to our house at Brownsville, Texas. Out stepped a preacher by the name of T. H. Lott whom we had never heard of previously. Since we had been using large quantities of Gospel tracts in Spanish in Mexico, he had gotten our name and address from the Pilgrim Tract Society of Randleman, South Carolina. He quickly explained why he had come to visit us. He told us that he was looking for a Christian Mexican wife since he considered the American women were generally speaking, too lazy and spoiled. It must have been the hand of God because we knew of a young, single Christian lady in the interior of the state of Tamaulipas in NE Mexico. Her name was Victoria Zavala and she was still living with her family in the small rural village named Ejido Pancho Villa, Tamaulipas. We had already helped to build a small church building made of the wattle (mesquite sticks) and daub (adobe mud plaster) type construction. We furnished the sanctuary with the 35-wooden folding chairs leftover from my Florida tent ministry and some benches we constructed.

The people commonly used kerosene lamps and we used Coleman gas lanterns since there was no electricity in these rural villages. The people had no running water in this village as was the case in many other rural villages in the early 1960's and drew water from hand-dug wells or carried water from ponds by hand or by hauling water in 55-gallon drums on burro drawn carts. Outhouse toilets in many areas of Mexico were the rule and not the exception. A young Christian girl from Brownsville, Texas by the name of Mary Martinez accompanied us as our interpreter. We had become well acquainted with Victoria's family since they had become some of the principle elements of the Pancho Villa Ejido Church. The Mexican people in these rural villages used donkeys, horses and even ox- carts to transport their harvests from their fields to their homes and markets. They also used the rural commercial bus system and trains in order to get to the bigger cities and markets.

The Zavala Family was very poor and Victoria had seen some hard circumstances but they really loved and served the Lord. God carried these faithful believers through the hard times. We arranged a trip to Mexico in our pickup truck with camper and took Bro. T. H. Lott with us to visit the work in Pancho Villa. We picked up Victoria and her two brothers who were preachers, and proceeded on to Ciudad Victoria, the capital city of the state of Tamaulipas. From there, we continued on across the mountain range into the high mountain plateau country where we had already established some preaching stations in several villages. We were gone on this trip for several days during which time, Lott and Victoria had gotten acquainted. When we arrived back in Brownsville, Bro. Lott found a house to buy and it wasn't long before they were married and settled down in Brownsville. Brother T. H. Lott was a certified welder and he traveled around with his new family, working on construction in Texas and Louisiana. At one time, I worked as his welder's helper at the Union Carbide Plant at Brownsville. Brother Lott accomplished many evangelistic objectives in the missionary work in Mexico and has gone on to be with the Lord. Sister Victoria is still living the Christian life along with her daughter and has always been a great blessing to us all.

In 1964, we helped Brother Lopez move from Ciudad Victoria over to the neighboring state of Coahuila, which was much more of a desert climate. They settled in the mountain village of Ejido Fraustro where his in-laws lived. This was about 40-miles north of Saltillo on the road to Monclova. There we built our first mission church in that region. At this time, Brother Lopez did some walking to reach neighboring people with the Gospel. In addition, he had a sturdy Mexican bicycle for transportation and he would ride to different villages. One time he told of being chased by a bull on his way to one of the more distant mission churches. When Sister Pearl

Carter in Williston, Florida heard about Bro. Lopez only having a bicycle to ride, she donated $300.00 to start a fund to buy him a pickup truck for his family and the ministry. Adele and I added to the fund and continued receiving money until we had a thousand dollars. We took Brother Lopez to the large city of Monterrey to look for a truck and found one in reasonably good shape and purchased it. Since Brother Lopez hadn't yet learned to drive, another Christian brother drove it back to Fraustro and he returned to Monterrey on the regular train that came through Fraustro from Durango. We had a dedication service for the truck, and then I had the job of teaching Brother Lopez how to drive the pickup. After he learned the ropes of driving, I taught him how to regularly service and maintain the vehicle. He learned very quickly how to fix flat tires, change spark plugs, grease all the joints, change oil and filters, work on the brakes, and so on. Not long after this, a friend in Georgia donated a motor to install in the pickup and Brother Lopez drove the truck to the border and we installed the new engine.

Now, the Lopez family could all go to church meetings in other towns and villages together and this really helped the work in the Coahuila region. We only helped him to evangelize the desert region north of Saltillo, Coahuila and consequently, we helped to build five missions as God added to the Church through our combined efforts. Our evangelical outreach was mostly in rural settings although we did some evangelistic work in urban and metropolitan areas. The next mission church we built was at Ejido La Tortuga or the Turtle soon followed by the third and largest of the missions built at nearby Ejido San Cosme. This sanctuary had the only galvanized metal roof. We had tried to build a church at Ejido Alto de Norias but the village elders and people were staunch Roman Catholic and refused us the permission to get started. God wanted a sanctuary to be built there for the few Evangelical believers that had come to the Lord. We were having street meetings in this village on Saturdays and one Saturday when we arrived, we were notified that an 8-year old girl who had been playing on the street with her friends was struck and killed by lightening. We postponed the meeting and instead, visited the grief stricken home of this little girl out of respect for the family. Her small body was lying in the simple casket just as she had died with no make up or embalming. When we came in, I could tell that it was having an effect on the girl's family. The grandfather asked Brother Lopez to say a prayer. He not only prayed but also preached a sermon in a very plain and tearful way under the anointing and power of the Holy Spirit of God. We manifested our sympathies and condolences to the family of the deceased and left.

The next day, the village fathers and elders got together for a meeting. We found out that they had decided to let us build a church sanctuary on any lot we chose in the village and we didn't waste any time. We chose a spot at the entrance of the village and erected an adobe structure with a cement floor, wooden window shutters and door, and with a built up roof typical of the area. All these many years, God has blessed this church and the village. I only wish we could visit there more often. The fifth mission sanctuary of the region was constructed several miles off the paved highway at Ejido El Pellial. Brother Julio Medina and his wife were caretakers and overseers there for a while. There is a new mission church further down the highway at La Paloma. We have helped in a small way to help this church get started. We thank God for this church because we had been to La Paloma several times in the past to conduct evangelistic meetings in the open air.

Brother Jose Lopez accompanied Silas and I on a mission trip from Saltillo through the states of Zacatecas, Jalisco and Colima to the west coast of Mexico in 1977. We visited Brother Lopez's hometown of Buenavista in Jalisco and preached and gave out Gospel literature on the streets, in homes, in churches and town parks as well as in jails and penitentiaries all along the way. We continued working together in mission and pastoral work for the next 17-years until he passed away on June 13, 1978, at the age of 43 years. His grave is in a rural cemetery near the railroad station at Fraustro, Coahuila and his headstone bears the Spanish version of the Scripture from the Book of Job, chapter 19, verse 25. The English translation says: *"For I know that my Redeemer liveth, and that He shall stand at the latter day upon the earth"*. The New International Version renders the end of this verse as: *"...stand at the latter day upon my grave"*. (copyright- NIV) This precious Bible verse inspired the composer G. F. Handel to write his beautiful Number 45 of Messiah. Among other inspired fruits produced by this favorite verse is the old-fashioned Christian Hymn- "*I Know That My Redeemer Liveth*", written in 1893, by Jessie Brown Pounds with music adapted to the song in 1917, by Christian songwriter James H. Fillmore, Sr. (http://www. cyberhymnal.org) The verse's true meaning is that Jesus Christ is our personal savior and that He will be intimately involved in the bodily resurrection of each born-again Christian that died in the faith. A good example of this is the case of the resurrection of Lazarus. Death surrenders to the Divine power of Jesus Christ and all the believers will greet the Resurrection and The Life in person as they come forth from their obsolete graves.

Brother Lopez, along with myself and others, had actively sowed the good seed of the Gospel in that good ground and now it is bearing fruit. Over the years, different preachers from Georgia, Indiana, Arkansas, Mississippi, Minnesota and the good old Lone Star State of Texas have come down to Mexico with us to visit, preach, minister or help in some way. Many friends and a few relatives have manifested an interest in our ministry but it is strange indeed how others have no interest whatsoever in reaching the lost sheep.

After over 45-years of ministering by faith to the un-evangelized, I know without the shadow of a doubt that the Almighty God wanted us in Mexico. His specific plan and purpose was that we become missionaries to Mexico, preaching the Gospel and going about doing good to the Indigenous and Spanish-speaking people. It has been proven over and over that the door was and still is open to Mexico for the Gospel to be brought in. We left all of our material dreams and commercial plans in order to go to the mission field, specifically in Mexico. We left family, friends and a gasoline station along with our plans for the future in order to fulfill God's plan in our lives. We have never been supported by any religious denomination or church organization and yet we have accomplished the work of an evangelist and: "*I have fought a good fight, I have finished the course, and I have kept the faith*". (II Timothy 4:7) To put it pure and simple, this isn't insanity, this is Christianity!

Many times, different people have asked us about how we make a living. God was working it all out since even before Adele was saved. God knows the end from the beginning and when we let God have his way, He will supply all our needs. When I was discharged from the Army Air Force in 1945, I was awarded a 40% service connected disability veteran's pension. By the time I was sent to the Florida State Hospital in May 1958, things would change dramatically. After being at Chattahoochee for thirty days, the Veteran's Administration raised my veteran's disability compensation pension to 100%. The veteran's disability pension that I was fairly awarded along with Social Security has been a source of our economic income down through the years even to the present time. I have also worked on many different jobs to supplement our income and I thank the Lord for a conscientious Christian wife who has been very conservative and saving in every way. We have managed our financial assets very well based on the conviction of the Holy Spirit who leads and guides us in the way we should go and also based on the economic role models provided by Godly men such as John and Charles Wesley. Our goal of helping others has God's attention and he has blessed us for our careful financial management and conservative life style. I would like to reiterate that the ones responsible for sending me to the mental institution at Chattahoochee, apparently did it for revenge or for some other evil motive but our Heavenly Father, the Almighty God of Heaven and Earth, turned it around and made a great blessing out of it and I am still receiving the fringe benefits from the experience today.

Consequently, I have no hard feelings toward anyone or bitter thoughts or even regrets in the matter of experiencing the hellish place called Chattahoochee. By God's wonderful and amazing Grace, my heart is clear of hatred or malice. It was God's will for my life according to Roman's 8:28. When I speak of a possible revenge motive, I mean that when I was really saved, I was saved all the way. I was saved and baptized in the Holy Spirit of God and I lost sight of this sinful world and all of its temporal allurements. I quit smoking tobacco the same hour and I quit selling the nasty and deadly stuff three days later. This one dramatic change in my life made a lot of church going people very angry with me in spite of the fact that as a grown man, I had the perfectly legal and moral right *not* to use or sell a dangerous drug. I recall that even my Mother would complain that the smoke from Poppa's pipe would nauseate her. Now I am quite sure that she was allergic to tobacco smoke and was sickened by it many times but apparently she suffered in silence. Poppa preferred the George Washington brand of pipe tobacco and my selling it to him at wholesale price made him happy.

My conversion and subsequent theological differences with him over the doctrine of salvation coupled with the abrupt end of his cheap supply of pipe tobacco was the basis of Poppa becoming very angry with me for a protracted period of time. Those who became angry with me over the issues of theology and tobacco abuse included my wife, other relatives, some friends and some of my tobacco hooked in-laws. Some of these same beloved in-laws are now deceased, long before their time due to lung cancer and emphysema. For many years I prayed for them to be enlightened and I tried my best to warn everyone that would listen of the dangers of using alcohol and tobacco but to no avail- they hearkened not to the truth and went their foolish carnal way to an early grave and perdition. Several of my relatives would likely be enjoying life today had they heeded the warning to quit smoking cigarettes. My Mother-in-law in Branford, Florida even spit snuff at me from her front porch rocking chair for my bothering to warn her of the physiological dangers involved in dipping snuff. As humans, we aren't perfect and we oftentimes get into trouble when we don't follow Jesus. It is most unfortunate that some carnal believers are wrapped up in the bad habits of the world including alcoholism and smoking, dipping, and chewing tobacco products.

In terms of who we should follow, it little matters that Believers such as Charles Spurgeon smoked cigars in the past. I cannot follow Mr. Spurgeon in order to attempt to justify a bad habit. I follow the uncompromising Jesus Christ who never used tobacco or any other corrupting substance. In terms of habits, Jesus Christ and the Holy Apostles set the best possible example for all Christians to follow in all aspects of living. Consequently, I choose to follow the sinless, matchless pattern, perfect Son of God. The Lord had clearly called me to preach and of course I preached the Holiness message just as Jesus, the Apostles, the Wesley's, Billy Sunday and many other preachers of the Gospel. This is not a new message but is the same- Old, Old Story of Jesus and His Love! We must trust and obey God.

It is clear that my some in my family including friends and in-laws, only had a form of godliness oftentimes known in Evangelical lexicon as "churchanity". It is apparent that some of the family and in-laws felt that by sending me off to Chattahoochee, they could rid themselves of the negative stigma of an independent, non-denominational preacher in the small hometown community. The Gospel message that I preached discomfited the sinful lifestyles and less than spiritual practices, habits and religious theology of friends, family and strangers. I recall an occasion in 1973, when I visited my brother Quill in Florida. He had been among the first highway patrolmen in the state of Florida and in 1973, was stationed at Lake City. When I arrived, I parked my truck in the parking area. The truck had a large professionally painted sign on the side that read: *"Jesus Christ is Coming Soon, Please be Ready"* -Faith Gospel Mission. When he came in from patrolling and saw my truck with the sign, he must have cringed. He met me and told me to get into his car and he gave me a blunt lecture on the protocol of visiting him. He was very upset over the sign on my truck and informed me to only visit with him at his home and then only after calling him to make an appointment to visit. I felt uncomfortable with my brother's reaction to my visit in spite of the fact that Quill made no grandiose profession of being a Christian and insofar as I know, did not attend any church. This wasn't the only person nor the only time that the Gospel signs on my truck or on our property elicited a negative response. The scriptures in Matthew 10:33, Mark 8:38, and Luke 9:26, describe this scenario very well. Jesus said that whosoever is ashamed of Him and His words will be cause for the reciprocation of His shame for them when He comes in the glory of His Father with the holy angels.

Apparently, all that many members of my family have known in modern times has been a form of religion based on joining the church after the external ritual of water baptism. The popularized perception is that this is what constitutes salvation but this theological belief falls far short of the Biblical standard of truth. Satan has tricked many well-meaning and even highly educated people by falling for a religious experience instead of the new birth. Relatives and in-laws sent me to an insane asylum purportedly for me to recover my mind when I hadn't lost the sound mind of Christ that I acquired when my old life was changed to new life by the power of God. Besides, if an insane asylum is for any one, it would have to be a place for the feeble-minded, the criminally psychotic or those that have no presence of mind at all.

If Christians are to be considered eccentric or strange, it would be fair to acknowledge that Saint Francis of Assisi was known for manifesting some eccentric behavior. He was once observed preaching a topical sermon on the Love of God to a flock of birds. The Reformer-Martin Luther once threw an inkbottle at the devil and at a later time, an American General, Thomas J. Jackson avoided mailing letters if they were to be transported on Sunday or the Lord's Day. He personally prayed with African-Americans and donated significant sums of money to Black Sunday Schools when such devotion to helping slaves wasn't very popular. Bro. Robert Sheffey in Virginia was considered by some as being eccentric for his plain exercise of Faith and Pastor James Langley in Oklahoma prayed for his sick cows and God healed them. Such spiritual convictions are motivated by a real love for Jesus coupled with an implicit trust in God. They are sometimes desired as idealistic for personal living yet are considered to be eccentric, funny or strange today. If I had of followed suit, they surely would have performed a lobotomy on me. The fact will always remain that I was arrested and committed on the basis of preaching the Word of God to people who were desperately wicked and in need of Salvation. In reality, the only real accusation ever levied at me was phrased in the words of Dr. Curtiss: *"YOU, vast preeeching!"*. Someone obviously didn't like the plain preaching of the Word of God that Christ's love constrained me to deliver.

I have a great longing in my heart to see every one of those people who had anything to do with my being committed to a mental institution, become saved, sanctified and all their hearts made right with God before they leave this world. I sincerely believe that many of the people responsible for the sin of having me committed did so to some degree in ignorance of the fact that I could have been subjected to brain surgery or electric shock treatment, which would only have destroyed me as a person, a citizen and a human being. I could have died on the operating table of some strange so-called doctor like Dr. Curtiss or I could have been turned into some kind of permanent zombie or vegetable. I thank God for good health and a sound mind according to 2nd Timothy, 1: 7.

As we continued making trips into Mexico, others joined with us in the work from time to time. One precious couple in the Lord was Brother Carl and Sister Goldie Thomas of New Albany, Indiana who helped to build two of the five mission churches in Coahuila. Satan was always trying to hinder our work in Mexico. As our two youngest sons were growing up at Brownsville, they began to associate with the wrong crowd. Paul and Silas had developed musical talents and by the mid-1960's, decided to play rock music. They would go across the border to Matamoros to play music in the clubs, staying out real late at night and it got to the point that we couldn't handle them anymore. By the year 1970, I felt that the only thing to do was to sell the place at Brownsville and move over to a community named Brinson in South West Georgia. We continued to make trips from Georgia to Mexico but the distance was too great. In Georgia, we would visit in the home of Junior Wisham and others. At this time, Rodney was associating with our sons and playing in various rock and roll bands. Paul, Silas and Rodney turned out to be hippies and it wasn't long before Paul and Silas left home and went off to Atlanta to pursue their interests in rock music.

On May 20, 1973, Rodney Wisham was in a Gospel meeting and gave his heart and life to Jesus Christ and was set free from a sinful lifestyle. The very next morning, he came to our house and requested for me to baptize him. We got a group together and took him down to the Flint River and I baptized him in the old fashioned Gospel way. The next trip we made to the state of Coahuila in Northeast Mexico, Brother Rodney wanted to go as well as his sister Cathy and our son John. On this trip, I baptized my oldest son John and Cathy Wisham in a watershed arroyo called "El Rio Patos" or Duck River near the village of La Tortuga. Brother Rodney Wisham had a definite call to the evangelistic ministry, especially in Mexico. The Lord blessed us on this trip and when we returned to Georgia, Brother Rodney was already looking forward to the next trip.

It wasn't too long before we were headed back to the missions in Coahuila and since Brother Rodney was still a single man, he decided to stay in Mexico with the Lopez family in order to learn the Spanish language and to help out in the work. He helped Brother Lopez to construct the church sanctuary at Alto de Norias. My sons Paul and John were also involved in our missionary work in the state of Coahuila located in northeastern Mexico. Paul and his family made a trip to the main mission station at Ejido Fraustro, Coahuila in 1974, staying a month in order to help Brother Lopez and Brother Pablo Aguirre in ministry and outreach. John made several trips to help in the missions between 1973, and 1975. In June of 1974, Adele, John along with his family and I moved from Brinson, Georgia to the border at Weslaco, Texas and then landed in a small town near Laredo called Zapata. This has been our base of mission operations since that time until the present. Although we have slowed a bit in our activities due to the vicissitudes of age, Adele holds the home front as I continue making trips into the states of Tamaulipas, Nuevo Leon and Coahuila with Brother Rodney until this year, 2006, and I don't plan to quit any time soon.

EIGHTEEN

Workers in God's Vineyard

Rodney Wisham was about a year old at the time that I met the Wisham family in South West Georgia. I watched him grow up through the years of visiting with his family and the Father's Home community. He was converted when he was about twenty years old and I baptized him in the Flint River. He started going with us to Mexico to do missionary work in the state of Coahuila. Brother Rodney Wisham has played the guitar since he was a teenager. For over 30 years, he has accompanied my harmonica in church services across the United States and Mexico. When someone gets a blessing through our Gospel music, we get blessed as well since we don't play Gospel music for entertainment purposes.

Some time after Rodney Wisham's conversion, our son Silas moved from Atlanta, Georgia to Zapata, Texas on the border where we were living and in the late summer of 1976, moved to Los Angeles, California. In August, he was Born-Again and soon afterwards, he came back to Zapata to join with us in the missionary work. After living at Zapata for several months, he moved to Corpus Christi on the shore of the Gulf of Mexico where he lived as a guest at the Roloff Evangelistic Enterprises. Silas worked in construction and truck-driving jobs in the area in order to fund his way in the mission work. As a missionary evangelistic team, Brother Rodney, Silas and I have traveled many thousands of miles together in the

United States and Mexico and each one has played an important role in the mission endeavor in Coahuila.

In 1977, Silas, Brother Lopez and I made a trip across Mexico from Saltillo through Guadalajara and visited Bro. Lopez's hometown of Buena Vista, Jalisco. We continued on to the coast at Barra de Navidad where I baptized my youngest son- Silas in the Port of Manzanillo. After preaching along the tropical west coast we passed through the City of Colima on the return route. On two different trips through this large city, we preached to the inmates of the Colima State Penitentiary including some Americans held there on drug charges. Later, Brother Rodney and his family, Silas, Brother Aurelio from Ejido Fraustro and I made another trip following the same route through Guadalajara to the Pacific coast and back to Saltillo and the home mission at Fraustro.

We were all together for almost two months on an extended mission trip to the Yucatan peninsula of Mexico in 1978. It was on this trip that we made contact with Operation Mobilization with the ship Doulos berthed in the port of Veracruz. We teamed up with their evangelistic arm and conducted some intense local evangelism around the City of Veracruz. These evangelistic trips into the heartland of Catholic Mexico were some of our finest hours in the work of the Lord.

In 1981, Silas and I made an extended mission trip out to Douglas, Arizona to start scouting the mission field in Northwestern Mexico from that point. Our evangelistic trip into the states of Sonora and Sinaloa lasted for about three months. We spent quality time evangelizing among the Seri, Yaqui and Mayo Indians on the beautiful west coast of Sonora and Sinaloa preaching the Word of God, showing Gospel films, praying for the sick and afflicted, distributing Bibles, Gospels, tracts and illustrated Christian literature such as the illustrated Chick tracts and comics.

While we were in the city of Obregon, Sonora, I was involved in a bad auto wreck. I was injured with some fractured ribs and bruises and lost my best overhead camper in the encounter with a speeding Pepsi-Cola delivery truck. My pickup truck was severely damaged in the crash although repairs were made after my physical recovery and I ended up driving it out of Sonora and back to Zapata,

Texas at a later time. We met many Holy Spirit filled Christians and we had wonderful Christian fellowship as well as much success in evangelism during this trip. We visited several places that had not been evangelized and did some intense evangelistic work among the Yaqui tribe with Wycliffe Bible Translator John Dedrick in the Vicam area. Silas stayed in Douglas, Arizona to begin a pioneer missionary evangelistic work in the northwest region of Chihuahua and Sonora. He evangelized much of the region of the Yaqui Indian reservation in Southern Sonora in a four-year period of time. Silas and his son Aaron traveled extensively by bus and train in the mountain regions of the states of Chihuahua as well as Sonora. He was married in June 1983, and pastored an evangelical church in Aconchi, Sonora for three years beginning in June of 1985.

Brother Rodney and I visited Silas and Abigail during their pastoral ministry at the Aconchi Evangelical Church and visited the mission work they initiated at Sinoquipe, Sonora. The work of the Lord in this remote mountain village of the Sonora River began in 1985, with Silas and Abigail starting Bible studies in the home of the Barrios family. The mission was challenged by religious persecution. The townspeople refused to allow any Evangelical Church to be constructed for some years until finally relenting when the religious rights guaranteed to the people by the Mexican Constitution were invoked and defended. The foundation was laid, cement block walls were laid up to the four-foot level and under the cover of darkness, some unknown evil persons busted all of the blocks and broke down the walls to the ground level. A meeting was held in the town and it was publicly decided that if the work on this church building were interrupted again, the full weight of the law would be brought to bear in favor of the constitutional guarantees of freedom of religion.

The Barrios family has continued to grow in the Grace and knowledge of Christ. As a consequence of the Gospel being brought to Sinoquipe on a consistent basis since 1985, Mr. Barrios, Sr. was saved before he passed on, several of the Barrios children and neighbors have been genuinely converted, the Gospel is still being preached and now there is a beautiful and spacious Christian Church building in this village. The faithfulness and power of God coupled with the faith of His saints in this village has proven that God is still working in Mexico.

The mission work in Coahuila is ongoing and we still have three churches that are active as well as other preaching stations in homes. Brother Pablo Aguirre, the father-in-law of Jose E. Lopez, passed away at the age of 89 years in June 2005, and was buried at the Estacion Fraustro cemetery. He had worked with us in the mission work for 41 years as a native pastor and an evangelist. In June of 2005, we conducted a marriage ceremony and baptized the newlywed couple and another convert at Fraustro. A recent visit to Ejido La Tortuga allowed us to distribute significant amounts of food and clothing to needy persons and the church building was full to capacity. Brother Braulio, the long-time pastor at La Tortuga has become half blind with cataracts and is due to have an operation. A number of the native brethren in the rural villages are carrying on the leadership of the missions. In spite of many serious problems facing Mexico, in spite of the tyranny in Cuba, and in spite of the materialism in America, the Gospel is still being preached, lives are being changed, souls are getting saved, and the true Church of God is moving forward in Faith, Love and Power. I conclude in re-affirming that the main purpose of my writing this book is that souls will be saved and come to know Jesus Christ as Savior, Lord and Master. I pray that God will use my testimony so that a great many well-meaning church-going people will come to know the difference between "churchanity" and real salvation. This issue is a matter of life and death.

We must be born-again of the Holy Spirit and God will write our names in the Lamb's Book of Life. First, we must understand that we are completely lost and then tell God about our troubles. If it is from our sincere heart, just a simple prayer is all we need. If you have read this book and are not saved or you are not sure of your salvation, please pray with me from your heart:

"Dear God up in heaven, I come to you as a lost wandering sinner in need of help. I have been going my own way like a lost sheep. I am tired of wandering and living in sin like the Prodigal Son. I have tried everything and find no rest for my soul and I am willing to be a servant in your house where there is peace and joy

and love unspeakable. Dear God, please forgive me for waiting for so long, forgive me of all my sins and make me pure. Fill me with your Holy Spirit of power and give me a sound mind. I want to be ready when Jesus returns for His Saints. In Jesus' precious name, Amen". If I am writing to some one who has been saved and has left their first love, please repent and ask God to forgive you and come back home. Please allow God to intervene in your life through his son- Jesus Christ. God is waiting for all the prodigal sons and daughters to come and fellowship at His table spread with a sumptuous feast.

"Say not ye, there are yet four months, and then cometh harvest? Behold, I say unto you, lift up your eyes and look on the fields for they are white already to harvest." (John 4:35)

<u>Excerpts from Rev. Thomas Griffin's Journal:</u>

The period between the 18th or 19th year of my life, the impression made on my mind by my mother's example and up to the occurrence that led me to hear the Methodists fully, in the 25th year of my age. My mother (Mary Ann Andrews, born 2-14-1754 in VA, married John Griffin in Virginia on 11-19-1772,—died11/1814 in GA) *had been strong particularly for the Methodist people as the most of her relatives were of that order. She was not connected to them, I have thought because of my father cooling off to that order. She was a regular reader of the Holy Scriptures, oft did I see her in her private devotions and oft did I turn away and shed tears and vow to the Almighty that I would serve Him at an opportune period. From my earliest recollection: after the business of the house was over, she used to read in her Testament and close, by kneeling at her bed side- the efforts of the day. The truth I believe was this, her attachment was to the Methodist people and my fathers' to the Baptist. The house was divided... little did she ever dream that she was raising*

191

and advising sons to serve God through Jesus Christ, that were to travel as many thousands of miles by land and water as I have done to propagate that religion she so ardently was impressing on my mind. Shall it be my lot to rescue her name from oblivion? She has long since sunk into the grasp of death."

"I do most sincerely believe that the cross she bore on earth has borne her through the gloom of death to that rest remaining for the pious of every age and time and place. Oft in the midst of trials and troubles, when my hopes have been sinking, repeatedly has contemplation soared up to the havens of rest and figured in my imagination. A mother bending from the lofty abode above, looking to this world of sorrow that she once dwelt in and had to struggle through and witness how I resist and waged a warfare with those things that impeded my progress. The reflection has armed my mind for the conflict and I have been urged onward. If what I am penning should ever meet the eyes of a mother, let me exhort them never to be discouraged. A mother exercises an influence that a father does not." (Griffin, p. 40, 41)

<u>Note</u>: My fourth great-grandmother- Mrs. Mary Ann (Andrews) Griffin lived an exemplary Christian life and as a worker in God's vineyard, was an inspiration to her children. During her lifetime in Virginia and in Georgia, Mrs. Mary Ann Griffin was a blessing to her immediate family, to her spiritual community and to her extended family. The caliber of such women of faith is measurable in their own lives and in the tensile strength of the moral fiber manifested in their progeny. Mrs. Mary Ann Griffin's model culture at home and in public, was one of moral and spiritual fortitude. It is evident that she wielded an influence profoundly impacting her offspring and succeeding generations in America. She died in the Christian faith; she is in her immortal home rejoicing with the holy angels and her memory is held dear by our Griffin family. May God grant the favor that her gracious, motherly example of pious Faith, undying hope and sincere love be a witness of God's Grace to the world at large as she was to her own children. Her faithful light has shone through the strata's of time and beyond the confines of history to illuminate these pages. God be praised. (Silas Griffin, '06)

Leaving Georgia and going to the circuit called Brunswick- part in North and part in South Carolina in the year 1811—

"It was my lot this trip to travel from Georgia to my work with a Bro. McEwan, a neighbor of my father's. I traveled on down by the Grassy Islands on the Pee Dee, then on through Fayetteville, then down the Cape Fear River to the circuit. I began my work at Bro. Alexander Kings. In a day or two, Bishop Asbury came along. He looked at me with his English eyes under one of those peculiar squints and looked like he was drawing a bead on me. He asked me where I was born, I told him – Virginia and raised in Georgia. He conversed with me. In fact I was so conscious of my inferiority for the office and place I was and thought I would be glad he would not examine me too close. After dinner, he pursued his journey and leaving the family, he put his arms around me and bid me farewell. I was surprised at it as I was an awkward, rough-hewed, backwoods raised Georgian." (Griffin, p. 70, 71)

Note: (In early 1815, Thomas Griffin was visiting on the Opelousas circuit in Louisiana just after the battle of New Orleans. Thomas encountered groups of local Militia gathered in self-defense and at a place called New Town, LA; he met a man having the authority to stop all strangers. *"I told him who I was and showed my parchment from Bishop Asbury."* (Griffin, p. 100)

Spring 1812, On the Quachita Circuit, Louisiana
"In a month or two after reaching here, Bro. Drury Powell came up to see me and soon after his return to his labor, I received a letter from him that a rumor had reached Red River that an insurrection had taken place… and the people had come and ordered him off and threatened him with the whip and he was going to leave and thought all had better leave the country. I wrote to him we were Americans and my father and uncles were veterans in the Revolution. I felt myself innocent, I was under the protection of the laws of the state, the general government and the majesty of Heaven and I should stand my ground until the end of the year and advised him to stay but he thought it most prudent to leave and did so." (Griffin, p. 87)

A visit in Georgia

"In the fall of 1819, I was elected to attend the general Conference at Baltimore. In February 1820, John Lane and myself set out. We were to travel through Georgia, the Carolinas, Virginia and to Baltimore. I went on to Oglethorpe, visited with my brother John Griffin. The evening before I go there, I call and stayed with Sister Barnett. It was dark before I got there. I came somewhat unexpected on her. I do declare, so was my feeling affected I could not speak for some time. I did not wish to break out into a cry. After a while, my emotion subsided and I spent the night comfortable, talking over with her the various changes I had passed through since I left Georgia last. The next day I went to Brother John Griffin. Visited the graves in the evening of my parents and indulged in such thoughts and feelings such a scene is calculated to inspire. I visited some of the old acquaintances and some of my relatives. I left Brother John, after Lane came, we passed on. I preached Griffin Hubberts (or Hubbards) funeral, a son of a sister of mine. From Hubberts, Lane and myself set out for Baltimore." (Griffin, p. 86)

New Year, 1843

"I have commenced reading Blackstone's Communications Volume II on English jurisprudence and it is astonishing to think how I am delighted with the work. I believe I shall derive a benefit from it. I had not got through it before I was offered Clark & Lewis Travel to Columbia River. I have read them and Mango Parks Travels in Africa. Now in the 56th year of my age, I rise at 3 or 4 o'clock and read until light, then to work and by dark I can hardly walk I am so much worn down....few of us are up to this ingenious age." (Griffin, p. 172, 202)

"September 24, 1843- This day I am fifty-six years of age and nearly 31 years I have spent in the Southwestern parts of the United States, a climate hostile to the existence of man. How often have I been heated and cooled, wet and dried, how often in hunger and thirst, traveling by land and water. I have slept in fine houses and huts, in camps and often in the woods on a blanket with my saddlebags under my head. Oft in sickness and in health, often in dishonor and

never in honor except by a few plain devout people, repeatedly cast down but I am not destroyed. The young men who came out from the Southern states with me are long since gone. A mysterious Providence has kept me on the stage of life. Not a man of the old stock of preachers that I met are living but William Winans and dear Lord, what frightful havoc has death made in 30-years. They are nearly all swept away.

I this day feel that I am not able to describe the obligations I am under to the Great Preserver and deeply regret I am no more sensible of it than I am sensible. I prefer being at home with my family and shall be willing to think I shall be satisfied if I can see my debts paid and plain food and apparel the balance of my days. I shall bow to the dispensations of Providence and follow the best Lights I have. May that God whom I have tried to honor in the new and wicked parts of the United States keep me in his Holy keeping and preserve me from rashness and permit me to live a few years longer and if I am called hence, may he dispose of my children and save them from sin and the vices of this world." (Griffin, p. 182, 183)

"In the month of February 1845, I settled up all my dues to a fraction of debt and still had some money in hand. I felt as if a great burden was rolled from me. For several years I had contemplated at looking at east Florida. So I concluded I would go through Georgia and visit my relations that I had not seen for 25 or 28 years. Our staple commodity cotton was sunk so low I thought I would go and see if there was a place where I could have me a stock and raise sugar and cultivate the tropical fruits. I set out on the 24 of July 1845, from Mississippi and passed through Alabama and on the 12th day, reached my brother John Griffin in Coweta County, Georgia. I spent a few days with him and we set out together to visit a brother William and a sister who I had not seen in 28 years. When we met, I should not have known either of them and they in turn declared they would not have known me, such had been the alterations produced in 28 years in our appearance. I spent a few days very comfortable with them. I then set out for Florida. (on the return trip on a Monday evening) *I reached my brother William, spent a day with Sister Barnett and the next day started for Mississippi. Reached my*

brother John's and on the eleventh day, reached home and found the family in tolerable health." (Griffin, p. 195)

Excepting a number of references in a few out of print books dealing with the history of Methodism, some extant conference minutes from long years past, the essay by Bishop Galloway, some Griffin family Bible records, some census and tax records; precious little has been recorded or published about our ancestor, the Rev. Thomas Griffin. The memory of his life and ministry had almost passed into the dust bin of history and oblivion. We acknowledge the dedicated genealogical research done by Amy Thigpen which led Silas to the book- A History of Methodism by Rev. John G. Jones. In his book, a number of references to the appreciable Christian ministry of Rev. Thomas Griffin were found. This in turn led to the essay written in 1903, by Bishop Charles Galloway wherein he references and quotes directly from the hand-written, manuscript Journal by Thomas Griffin. After a protracted search for the Day Book and Journal, Silas found it at the MDAH in Jackson, MS in June of 2003, and obtained a copy to study and transcribe.

Rev. Thomas Griffin was a plain "Saddlebags" preacher, not a fancy "money bags" preacher. By a consensus, his Journal is a unique document. It is a historical, genealogical and spiritual treasure that speaks to people's hearts across the 155 years since the demise of Rev. Thomas Griffin. He dedicated his Journal to his children and desired that they publish it. Apparently, the only public exposition of any content of the Journal has been in the essay by Bishop Galloway, at www.griffin-lanning.com and in this book. It is our sincere desire that the quotes and excerpts from this "Saddlebags" Methodist preacher's Journal be a blessing to your heart. This is precisely what Rev. Thomas Griffin intended during the decade he spent in writing it.

Epilogue

Our view of the creation, the world and the universe could be put into musical terms. It is possible that God's simple yet symphonic plan for the universe is like this: The "Big-Bang" was the joyous opening note of an exciting and rousing eternal symphony and the Redeemed are the melodious never-ending stanzas of Godly praise. The Godly Patriarchs, Prophets, Apostles and Believers of all ages are useful instruments in the expert loving hands of the Creator. It is indisputable that God uses human and angelic instrumentality on a planetary scale to fulfill his divine plan and purpose. We simply cannot improve upon God's plan for the ages. His plan is perfect.

The loving fatherly God that we serve continues to call all men to repentance, to be Born-Again, and as such, into a close spiritual fellowship as members of God's family. The harvest fields are white already and some laborers are working in His fields while it is yet day. In spite of the vicissitudes of age and the high mileage on this mortal frame, my thoughts are constantly to be about The Father's business until I cross over the river to rest at the feet of Jesus in the shade of the Tree of Life. The Lord Jesus has been merciful to me throughout my life and my desire is to be a faithful Christian witness at every available opportunity.

I am now serving my third tour of duty. My first was in the Civilian Conservation Corps from 1933, to 1935, with rating as Survey Party Leader making $45.00 monthly under President Franklin Delano Roosevelt. The second tour was from 1942, to 1945, in the United States- Ninth Army Air Force with rank of Corporal. I served my country, lost my teeth and was awarded a disabled veteran's pension. My third tour of duty began with membership in God's family on March 15, 1950, continuing to the present day with honorable rank of "Good and Faithful Servant." My pay for this final tour of duty is Eternal Life. God's army is strictly a volunteer corps and He drafts no one. No conscripts serve in the Church Militant that is strictly guided and led by the Holy Spirit. I expect no day of separation from this mighty heavenly host, only an eventual promotion. The victorious Saints of God will go marching in the gates of pearl in the grandest victory parade ever, marching on the streets of gold past God's throne, endlessly singing and shouting praises to Jesus Christ our Lord. As Brother James Langley used to shout: *"By God's Grace, I'm planning on being there!"* How about you?

And so it is with every real child of God. There really is a closer walk with God. John the Beloved was not a personal favorite of Christ; he was simply a more fervent disciple. Jesus loved all the disciples and John loved the Christ with all his heart, mind and soul and his neighbor as himself. In stark contrast, throughout the entire Dispensation of Grace, some disciples follow Jesus from afar off. It is critically important that we follow Jesus Christ in a close personal relationship in order for us to completely trust and obey Him. Jesus Christ is a cultural, historical, and spiritual figure on the world scene and the Ecclesia or Church is founded upon Him. It is critically important that we maintain a viable connectedness to a historical Christianity since cultural and historical roots help validate the Church's future in an unstable world. There is no room in the Church for anti-Semitism, bitterness, discord, hatred, or persecution.

The Holy Scriptures declare in the Epistle of James, chapter 2, verses 17 and 18: *"Even so faith, if it hath not works, is dead, being alone. Yea, a man may say, Thou hast faith, and I have works; show me thy faith without thy works, and I will show thee my faith by my works"*. A classic example of the argument of a professed Faith standing alone is found on page 108 in Rev. Thomas Griffin's Journal. In 1815, he had stayed at Nachitoches for several days and had preached on a Sunday to a few people. Afterwards, *"One of the United States soldiers asked me to come and baptize a child of his, after dinner I did so. He appeared to make many efforts to make me believe he was friendly. He had procured several kinds of spirits and wines to make a good, agreeable baptizing time of it. He appeared to be astonished that I would not drink. After he had taken a few glasses, he told me he had listened to me that day and his religion and mine was just alike. I told him if we have good faith, we must have good works. His lady said: "Good faith was all that could be maintained; in a faith- good works would have to be given up." I thought, this is the creed of a great many"*! The truth of the matter is that faith without works is dead. I'm afraid that much of modern religion is a case of dead works involving dead hands on dead heads. God will deal with the dead branches.

On another occasion when he was preaching a two day meeting in one of the frontier settlements of the Opelousas circuit near the southern coast of Louisiana, Rev. Thomas Griffin delivered this sermon: *"I began by telling them- the Almighty had made all men, knew how to address Himself to all, and would hold all accountable, and there was neither time nor place that would dissolve the obligation. These facts I conceived, was impressed on the conscience of all men, both civilized and savage but men frequently shut their eyes against the light and become violators of the laws of God. The violation of the laws of God led to the violation of the laws of man and when man became a violator of the laws of society, that very law that was the safeguard of men, outlawed them and many learned by sad experience those great truths. Some men by their conduct brought themselves into notice"*. (Griffin, p. 109) This statement is so true. I think Thomas Griffin was simply reiterating the truth found in Scripture and the message he preached is still true and applicable. *"By faith, Abel offered unto God a more excellent sacrifice..... God testifying of his gifts; and by it he being dead yet speaketh."* (Hebrews 11:4) He being dead- yet speaks.

Any apostasy found in Christ's Church is a rebellion against God's truth and grace and it is purged. Dead branches can never produce fruit. Make sure that the road you travel on through this life, Roman road or otherwise, is doubtless conducting you to heaven and not to hell. Make absolutely sure that you have the old time religion; the kind that makes a Baptist love a Methodist, the one that

God has given us in order for us to love everybody unconditionally. Only God can give us this faith, hope and love.

Pastor Jose Ernesto Lopez of Mexico often quoted the directive found in the Gospel of Matthew, chapter 28, and verses 18-20. He preached fervently many times on the topic of the great missionary command given by Jesus Christ himself: *"All power is given unto me in heaven and in earth. Go ye therefore and teach all nations, baptizing them in the name of the Father, and of the Son, and of the Holy Ghost: Teaching them to observe all things whatsoever I have commanded you; and lo, I am with you always, even unto the end of the world"*. If the devil accuses us of preaching the Gospel, we can rejoice in the fact that we are doing exactly what God has called us to do. Let the heathen rage and let the chips fall where they may. Shallow believers and religious fanatics sometimes hurt and mitigate the public witness of Christianity but our sovereign God is still on His Holy Throne. God has never deviated from His eternal plan for humanity. God has never taken any right or left turns and the road to God is straighter than anything on planet earth.

Sin is the culprit to blame for all sorrow, suffering and death. It is never hateful, rude or unfair to blast the sin, to love the lost and to heal the sinner. God has mandated that Christians warn the wicked and has ordained believers to point the lost sheep to Jesus Christ, the True Shepherd of our souls. The harvest is the Lord's and He will separate the tares from the wheat and the chaff from the priceless grain and the Lord's holy granary will be filled with a righteous multitude without number. It is quite true that the gates of hell shall never prevail against the real Christian Church. The angels and multitudes of souls worship the true God and the saved of earth praise Him alone who was found worthy and who is above all. All is indeed peaceful and well in God's heavenly Kingdom. God is Omnipotent and is in full control.

In the end, what will you do with Jesus Christ?

Jack Ray Griffin   Silas Griffin

Magna est veritas et praevalet.
"Great is truth, and it prevails"

BIBLIOGRAPHY

Ball, T.H., Rev. *A Glance into the Great South-East, or Clarke County Alabama* Grove Hill, AL 1879 (Reprint- Clarke County Historical Society, Grove Hill, AL 1994)

Baldwin, Leland. D. *The Keelboat Age on Western Waters* Pittsburg University of Pittsburg Press 1941

Barbery, Willard S. *Story of the Life of Robert Sayers Sheffey* Salem, OH Schmul Publishing Co., Inc. Weslyan Book Club

Carr, Jess *The Saint of the Wilderness* Radford, VA Commonwealth Press, Inc. 1974

Caselaw 50 Pivotal Cases – "O'Connor v. Donaldson" 422 U.S. 563 (1975) (original documents at: <http://www.findlaw.com> <www.caselaw.lp.findlaw.com>) <http://www.aclumontana. org>

Chattahoochee Director-Mick Jackson Producers-John Daly & Derek Gibson HBO Video Videocassette Hemdale Film Corporation New York 1990

Clayton State University "Mens rea & Actus rea" 2005 <http://www. tech.clayton.edu> Morrow, GA

Cornell University Law School "Mens rea, Actus rea" http://www.law.cornell.edu 2005 (Content available under a Creative Commons Attribution-ShareAlike 2.5 license)

Cragg, Gerald R. (Editor) *The Works of John Wesley*, Vol. II The Appeals to Men of Reason and Religion and Certain Related Open Letters, Nashville: The Abingdon Press, 1989 (From Jackson's Edition of Wesley's Journal— (Public Domain)

Cyberhymnal "The Love of God" by Fred Lehman and "I Know That my Redeemer Liveth" by Jessie B. Pounds and James H. Fillmore <http://www.cyberhymnal.org> 2006 (Public Domain)

Davis, William C. *A Way Through The Wilderness: The Natchez Trace and the Civilization of the Southern Frontier* New York, NY Harper Collins Publishers, Inc. 1995

Donaldson, Kenneth *Insanity Inside Out* New York, NY Crown Publishers, Inc. 1976 (Maxwell Aley & Assoc. Paonia, CO) 2006

Editor "Society's Warehouses" *New York Times* Tuesday, November 12, 1974, Editorial section, page 38, col. 2

Florida State Archives *Inquisition of Incompetency records* Tallahassee, FL Section 394.4615 Florida Statutes 1958

Ellis, William T. "Billy" Sunday The Man and His Message Philadelphia, PA The John C. Winston Co. Pubs. 1914

Elliot, Elisabeth *Shadow of the Almighty The Life & Testament of Jim Elliot* New York Harper & Brothers 1956

Elliot, Elisabeth *Through Gates of Splendor* New York Harper & Row Pubs. 1957

Evans, A. R. *Sammy Morris* Grand Rapids, MI Zondervan Publishing House 1958

Florida State Hospital *Admission record* Chattahoochee, FL Section 394.4615 Florida Statutes 1958

Galloway, Charles H., Bishop "Thomas Griffin; A Boanerges of The Early Southwest" (essay) *Publications of The Mississippi Historical Society* Vol. II, Oxford, MS 1903 (Public Domain)

Griffin, Sam. M., Jr. (Editor & Publisher) "Photo of Missionaries from Mexico and Local Pastor" The Post-Searchlight Bainbridge, GA (B/W group photo in GA, ca. 1970)

Griffin, Thomas, Rev. *Day Book and Journal* 1841 (Call # Z/2079.000/S) Mississippi Department of Archives and History 200 North St. Jackson, MS 39205 (Public Domain 12/31/2002) (Quotes from the original Journal as transcribed by Robert Silas Griffin starting June 24, 2003, cited in text are used in this book by permission of MDAH) A part of the excerpts from the Journal in Chapter 18, are from the transcription done by Will Mary Simrall Pratt- 2000, and also by Robert Silas Griffin-2003—2006)

Hebert, Tim "Richmond Nolley" Archives & History....Louisiana Conference UMC Hist. Soc. <http://www.iscuo.org/nolley. htm> Copyright 1999—2000 (Referenced in 2005 / 2006)

Howard, Alton H. Publishing Co. "The Love of God" by Fred Lehman and "I Know that My Redeemer Liveth" -Jessie B. Pounds, James H. Fillmore W. Monroe, LA Howard Publishing Co., Inc. 1994 (Public Domain)

Hurlbut. Jesse Lyman, D. D. *Hurlbut's Story of the Bible for Young and Old* Chicago The John C. Winston Co. 1932

Isocrates *Orations* Vol. I, B. C. 380 (translated by J. H. Freese) London: George Bell & Sons 1894. (Public Domain)

Jones, John G., Rev. *A Complete History of Methodism* Vol. I Nashville, TN Southern Methodist Publishing House 1887 Vol. II Nashville, TN & Dallas, TX Publishing House of the Methodist Episcopal Church, South 1908 Copyright 1966 by Claitor's Book Store Baton Rouge, LA

Lanier, Sydney *Song of the Chattahoochee* Mary D. Lanier New York Trow's Printing and Bookbinding Co. Charles Scribner's Sons Copyright 1884 (Public Domain)

Malone, Randolph A. *Malone and Allied Families* Thomasville, GA 1996

McTyeire, Holland N., Bishop *A History of Methodism* Nashville, TN Publishing House of the Methodist Episcopal Church, South 1893 (Public Domain)

New International Version *Holy Bible* Colorado Springs, CO 1973, 1978, 1984

Orwell, George *Animal Farm* 1945 (Public Domain)

Perez, Adrian "Artwork #0131-321800" Douglas, AZ 2003

Smith, Betty James, and Rhonda Smith "Florida State Hospital, Chattahoochee, Gadsden County, Florida" <http://www.rootsweb.com/~flgadsde/fsh/> 2001 / 2006

Thompson, Frank Charles *The Thompson Chain Reference Bible* (KJV - 1611) Indianapolis, IN B. B. Kirkbride Bible Co. 1964

"The Constitution of the United States," Amendments- 1, 4, 5, 6, 8 and 14, Section 2

Watson, Charles Hoyt *DE SHAZER The Doolittle Raider Who Turned Missionary* Winona Lake, IN Light & Life Press 1950

Printed in the United States
67282LVS00012B/28-48

9 781600 344800